BY CAROL CONWAY & WILLIAM E. NOTHDURFT

BEST PRACTICE SERIES

THE INTERNATIONAL STATE

Crafting a Statewide Trade

Development System

The Aspen Institute
Rural Economic Policy Program

ISBN: 0-89843-186-7

COVER ILLUSTRATION ©THOMAS LOCHRAY, THE IMAGE BANK.
DESIGN AND PRODUCTION: BR PUBLICATIONS, WASHINGTON, DC.

TABLE OF CONTENTS

Section 1: The Need for an International State

Section 2: Becoming an International State

(Continued on next page)

Table of Figures

ACKNOWLEDGMENTS

The book draws on the co-authors' experience, spanning more than three decades, in state economic development policy overall, and in trade development in particular. It is the result of a lengthy review of state trade programs, and of personal interviews with state trade office staff and other trade assistance practitioners throughout the South and West. In addition, a day-long workshop involving rural development professionals helped illuminate the particular difficulties of improving the competitiveness of rural firms.

The authors wish to express their gratitude to the Rural Economic Policy Program (REPP) of The Aspen Institute for its early and unwavering support of this project. Meriwether Jones, director of REPP, and Janet Topolsky, associate director, were instrumental in helping us think through the rural policy implications of this book. Nancy Stark, who reviewed the proposal and served as our first project director, is also warmly acknowledged.

Funding for this project was provided jointly by REPP, with its support from the W.K. Kellogg Foundation, and by the U.S. Economic Development Administration (EDA). Over the years, EDA has been a pioneer in supporting research and innovation in state economic development and international competitiveness. Two EDA officials, Dave Geddes and Richard E. Hage, both recently retired, deserve special recognition for the role they played in advancing the field.

The authors would also like to acknowledge the sponsors and two dozen participants in the *Best Bets for Rural Trade* workshop held at the U.S. Department of Agriculture as part of this project. Todd Landfried and Dafina Williams of the USDA Extension Service were especially supportive in developing the workshop.

Preliminary manuscripts were reviewed by state trade and economic development officials and representatives of the U.S. Economic Development Administration, the Appalachian Regional Commission and the

National Association of State Development Agencies, among others. We are particularly grateful to these of the first draft reviewers: Mary Buckley, Diane Burke, William Miller, Hugh Nichols, Alison Porter and Elaine Stuart. Many others provided helpful comments. Special recognition is also due Peggy N. Barnard, founder and president of Barnard Global Corporation, who worked with the authors in the early stages of planning the book.

Thanks to Ronnie Kweller for editorial services, and Betsy Rubinstein of BR Publications for design and editing assistance. Finally, special thanks are also owed to Shireen Zonoun of the Corporation for Enterprise Development, who spent hours generating charts and drafts of the manuscript.

Readers of this book may want to consult a companion volume, *Internationalizing Rural Economies: Problems, Principles and Practice,* by William E. Nothdurft, also published by The Aspen Institute's Rural Economic Policy Program in its *Strategic Overview* Series.

All viewpoints expressed in this book are those of the authors and do not necessarily represent the official views of the sponsoring organizations.

"Who called the doctor?!" snapped an irritated state trade director upon learning at a meeting that state trade promotion programs were the subject of a new study.

His irritation was mixed with fear, bred from experience, for despite lofty pronouncements by politicians about the importance of competing in a global economy, state trade directors are a beleaguered bunch. To begin with, the priority given to state trade programs fluctuates constantly with the political winds. And tinkering is endemic. Indeed, tinkering—grafting a program here, tacking on an initiative there—is how most trade promotion programs have developed in the first place.

Despite lofty pronouncements by politicians about the importance of competing in a global economy, the priority given to state trade programs fluctuates with the political winds.

To complicate matters, the data available to state trade offices to assess and analyze trade performance in a region are limited and often unreliable. Partly as a consequence, trade staff have trouble documenting the results of their work. Moreover, they are seldom given clear performance objectives or program protocols, making performance measurement that much more difficult. Finally, a state trade office's constituency, though large, typically is mute and almost invisible.

Under these conditions, a certain defensiveness on the part of trade directors is understandable, perhaps even warranted. Nonetheless, there are unmistakable symptoms that the patient—trade assistance programs in America's states and regions—is in distress. A few of the leading signs:

■■ After experiencing strong growth for several years, state budgets for international business development have flattened in most states and declined in many—even as the challenge of international competitiveness has grown.

■■ In some states, legislative audits have raised serious questions about program performance.

■■ In others, business leaders interested in trade but frustrated with existing public programs are creating new private sector-led export service
organizations to meet needs they feel are unmet.

In
today's global economy,
the condition of the state's
trade assistance services will
determine to no small degree
the condition of the
state's economy and the
quality of the lives of the
state's citizens.

■■ In most states, there is neither a system for international policy and program development nor an effort
underway to develop a civic capacity for supporting
one.

■■ Perhaps most important, the number of firms
engaged in international business activities remains
modest. And even *among* exporters, the percentage
of total sales accounted for by exports typically is
small.

In states and regions across the United States, this ail-
ing patient deserves better than the primitive treatments
to which it has been submitted in the past. Significant and
lasting improvement requires advanced diagnostic tests
and aggressive therapies. For in a very real sense, in
today's global economy, the condition of the state's trade
assistance services will determine to no small degree the condition of the
state's economy and the quality of the lives of the state's citizens.

The Trade Imperative

"**G**lobal competitiveness" is not a vague economic abstraction, it is a
matter of economic survival. The Europeans have known this since the
Age of Discovery. The Asians are learning fast. The United States, however,
luxuriating in its huge domestic market, has been more than a little slow
on the uptake. But we no longer have that luxury. Even if our companies
don't seek overseas markets—and most don't—overseas competitors are
flooding ours. The issue could hardly be more basic: It's about money,
market share and jobs.

A 1995 study by the Institute for International Economics and The
Manufacturing Institute found that firms that export grow faster, create

more jobs, pay better, are more productive, fail less often, and innovate more rapidly than firms that do not export.[1] Exporting creates new sources of profits and company growth; diversifies the customer base, thus decreasing business cycle vulnerability; increases production economies of scale and, thus, profitability; and extends product life cycles. What's more, the study found that the benefits from export reliance are not limited to corporate elite, but touch everyone. The result? Stronger companies and stronger economies.

The States Take On Trade

Throughout the 1980s, states took on increasing responsibility for job creation strategies. The reason was simple: Even as federal outlays for economic development were stagnating or shrinking, recessions and industrial restructuring continued to throw an alarming number of Americans out of work.

In this challenging environment, states leaped upon export promotion as a relatively quick and inexpensive way to stimulate sales and job growth. In some ways, however, states' programs mirrored existing federal government activities, perhaps most visible in the duplicative network of overseas trade offices.

In the 1980s, states leaped on export promotion as a quick, inexpensive way to stimulate sales and job growth. In some ways, however, states' programs merely duplicated existing federal activities.

The leading states, which already had overseas offices devoted to recruiting foreign investment, began to tack on the additional responsibilities of arranging state trade missions, finding trade leads and matching state exporters to foreign agents and distributors. Nearly every state followed these leaders, with some devoting their overseas offices entirely to export promotion. Although the U.S. and Foreign Commercial Service and the commercial sections of some embassies already were offering the same kind of export promotion services, states did not feel the posts were adequately staffed and responsive. In addition, a measure of pride and a desire for confidentiality often drove states to set up this parallel network of overseas posts.

The issue of the central role of the state in trade development is not new. In 1989, the National Governors' Association (NGA), under the leadership of its then-Chairman, Virginia Governor Gerald L. Baliles, issued *America in Transition: The International Frontier*. In the report, Gov. Baliles challenged his fellow governors to bring an international perspective to daily living, to pursue emerging markets, and to reintroduce the spirit of the Yankee trader to American business. He concluded:

> *"Business as usual" just is not enough anymore. As the world gets smaller, state initiatives must become more far-reaching. The competition has gotten tougher, but American companies are in a good position as long as they act promptly. A statewide strategic trade plan, developed at a Governor's behest, can keep things moving... Governors should take immediate steps to develop such a plan. The changing international trading system, and our position in it, demand a strategic response. The challenges are real. The opportunities are great. The stakes are high. The time is now.[2]*

The changing international trading system, and our position in it, demand a strategic response. The challenges are real. The opportunities are great. The stakes are high. The time is now.

Actually, the timing could hardly have been worse; the states were broke. The release of the NGA report coincided with the state fiscal crisis of the early 1990s. Between 1984 and 1990, state international budgets had grown dramatically at a rate of 40 percent a year, rising from an average of $590,000 per state in 1984 to $2,025,000 in 1990. Initially, much of this money went toward recruiting foreign investment, but efforts to expand export opportunities gradually took precedence in most states as the 1980s ended. By contrast, between 1990 and 1992, state international budgets as a whole rose only 7 percent a year, and the export promotion portion actually fell by an average of 9 percent.[3]

In many states this fiscal austerity is likely to be a fact of administrative life well into the foreseeable future. But there is a silver lining of sorts: This very austerity has required states to look much more closely at both *what* they are doing about international trade and *how well* they are doing it.

Indeed, an independent study of public and private services reveals that the potential for states to serve as brokers and catalysts is a long way from being a reality. The Kenan Institute of Private Enterprise at the University of North Carolina surveyed a representative nationwide sample of small- and medium-sized exporting manufacturers, asking them two questions:

■■ To whom have you turned for any of 24 different export assistance services?

■■ Were the services offered by those providers of value?

The survey provides, for the first time, an empirical perspective on customer use of and satisfaction with trade services. But the results are not good. The 1995 study, called *A Report Card on Trade*, found that:

State trade offices have the potential to be the nexus of a comprehensive statewide trade development system. But they cannot do it alone.

> *State programs were the leading source for only one service, training to help exporters' staff handle export operations. They reached more than 5% of midsize exporters with valued assistance in only one area, how-to information, and did not reach this threshold with any service to small firms.*[4]

Toward a Statewide Trade Development System

The Kenan Institute does not speculate as to why state programs rank poorly. This book, however, does.

The central message of this book is that state trade offices have the potential to be the nexus of a comprehensive statewide *trade development system*. But, given their limited resources, they cannot alone assure the international competitiveness of a state's economy. They must be supported by a widely shared vision of the state's international future and must integrate public, private and nonprofit trade service providers into a coherent system for developing international business and assuring that its benefits are widely shared.

This book provides states with the tools necessary to rethink their trade assistance services and to create such a system to help businesses, communities and regions compete internationally. Examples of existing initiatives that embody aspects of a statewide trade development system are presented throughout the book.

To succeed in their trade development efforts, state trade offices must integrate public, private and nonprofit trade service providers into a coherent system.

SECTION 1 of this book describes the history and current status of what is commonly called "trade promotion" in the United States.

■■ CHAPTER 1 examines recent national trade performance, presents the rationale for creating effective trade assistance services, and describes the special challenges faced by rural firms and communities struggling to compete in a globalizing economy.

■■ CHAPTER 2 takes a close look at the current condition of state trade services.

■■ CHAPTER 3 explores the new conditions of state governance and the emergence of both new players and new rules in the world of export assistance.

SECTION 2 of this book presents a new way of organizing and delivering public and private sector trade assistance services in the context of a statewide trade development system.

■■ CHAPTER 4 explores the strategic issues involved, lays out eight basic principles to guide the creation of such a system, and contrasts the goals, strategies and relationships involved in current trade assistance services with those of a new, "second generation," statewide system.

■■ CHAPTER 5 broadens the scope of the discussion from trade services to the larger issue of strengthening a state's capacity to address a wide range of foreign policy issues and opportunities.

■■ *CHAPTER 6* presents a series of specific actions states can take to build the international awareness and capacity of all it citizens and institutions.

Finally, the *CONCLUSION* summarizes the objectives of the international state, outlines the basic design principles, lists the tools involved and identifies some issues to explore in the future.

CHAPTER 1. THE STATE OF TRADE IN THE UNITED STATES

In the waning weeks of 1994, the U.S. Congress, by surprisingly wide margins in both houses, ratified the General Agreement on Tariffs and Trade (GATT). Although few members were likely to have actually *read* the 22,000-page pact, congressional leaders and administration officials hailed its passage as a landmark event. Significant long-term economic growth and job creation were predicted as results of GATT's promise to create a more "level playing field" for international trade. Almost no one asked whether the United States had a team to put on that field. Someone should have.

Status Report: U.S. Exports and Export Promotion

The United States is the world's biggest exporter, but it is also the world's biggest export underachiever.[5] According to the U.S. Department of Commerce's Exporter Data Base, only 6.5 percent of all U.S. companies that had paid employment in manufacturing or intermediary trade enterprises (wholesalers, trading companies and the like) were direct exporters in 1987 (the most recent complete analysis).[6] And while the Commerce Department estimates that the number of exporting firms has grown since then, perhaps by as much as 20 percent, estimates of how these firms break down by size and level of export activity vary widely. Certainly, large firms dominate. In 1987, the nation's top 2,000 exporters accounted for 93 percent of the value of manufacturing exports.[7] In 1993, a mere 50 companies accounted for nearly half of the value of all U.S. exports.[8]

> The United States is the world's biggest exporter, but it is also the world's biggest export underachiever.

Yet it is the nation's small and medium-sized exporters that are the target of federal and state trade development decisionmakers, for several reasons. First, there are tens of thousands of them; second, they offer enormous potential for export growth; and third, the percentage of exports accounted for by large firms has changed little for years. A national survey of exporting firms in 1995 found that, compared to 66 percent of mid-sized firms (100-1000 employees), only 14 percent of smaller firms (20-100 employees) were direct exporters. Adding indirect exporting increased these figures to 80 percent of mid-sized firms, but only to 18 percent of smaller ones.[9] Adjusting for differences in the definition of small and medium-sized firms, these figures are roughly comparable to other recent surveys. The Commerce Department, for example, has estimated that half of all medium-sized firms (100 to 499 employees) and 10 percent of all small firms (under 100 employees) export. Combining small and medium-sized firms, Arthur Anderson and National Small Business United estimate that 25 percent of such firms export.[10]

The most disturbing news hides in the data not on the number of firms that export, but on the percentage of firms' total sales that are accounted for by exports. The most recent data suggest that, for 40 percent of medium-sized exporters, exports represent less than 5 percent of sales. For three-quarters of these companies, exports are less than 20 percent of sales. Moreover, only 17 percent of small firms have exports that exceed 20 percent of total sales.[11]

> **O**nly one in four companies that *could* export does so. And among those few firms that *do* export, export sales are only one-fourth of their potential.

The message is clear: while more firms are dabbling in the odd export, those that are committed traders are still a small minority. This fact alone goes a long way toward explaining why—whether one measures "exports as a percent of gross domestic product (GDP)" or "exports per capita"—the United States ranks at or near the bottom of the industrialized world in export intensiveness.[12] *(See Figure 1.)*

Thus, there are two issues at the heart of the problem of internationalizing American business. First, while not all firms are capable of exporting, it is estimated that only one in four companies that *could* export does so.[13] Second, among those few firms that *do* export, export sales are only one-fourth of their true potential.[14] In short, while the United States has a few export "stars," it doesn't have much of a team. Few firms export; of those that do, most ship so infrequently to so few places at such low

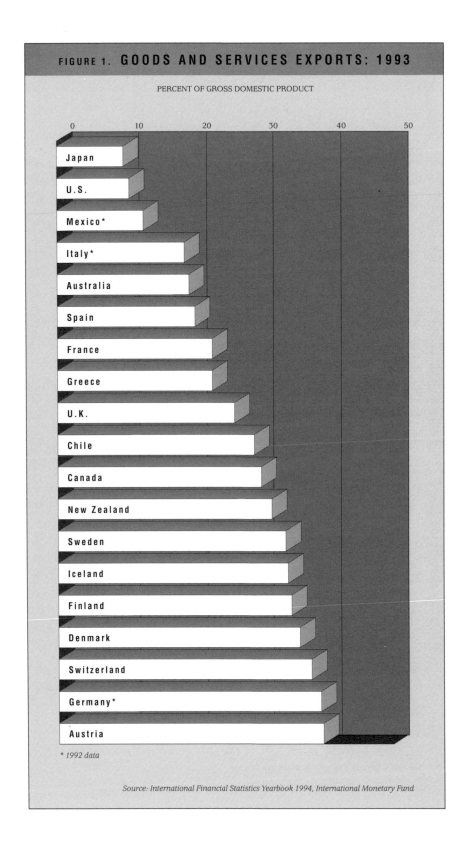

FIGURE 1. GOODS AND SERVICES EXPORTS: 1993

PERCENT OF GROSS DOMESTIC PRODUCT

0   10   20   30   40   50

Japan

U.S.

Mexico*

Italy*

Australia

Spain

France

Greece

U.K.

Chile

Canada

New Zealand

Sweden

Iceland

Finland

Denmark

Switzerland

Germany*

Austria

* 1992 data

Source: International Financial Statistics Yearbook 1994, International Monetary Fund

THE INTERNATIONAL STATE: CRAFTING A STATEWIDE TRADE DEVELOPMENT SYSTEM

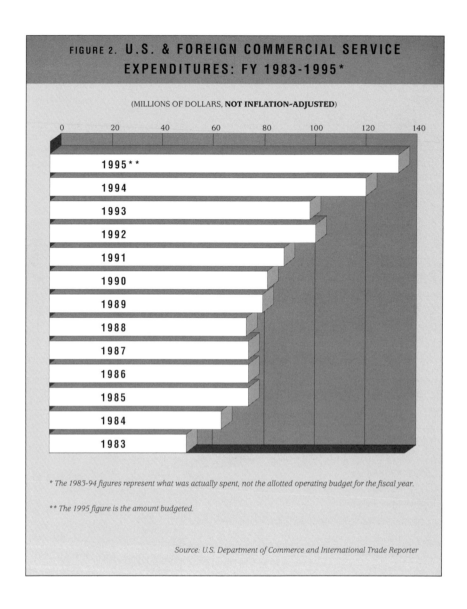

FIGURE 2. U.S. & FOREIGN COMMERCIAL SERVICE EXPENDITURES: FY 1983-1995*

(MILLIONS OF DOLLARS, **NOT INFLATION-ADJUSTED**)

1995**
1994
1993
1992
1991
1990
1989
1988
1987
1986
1985
1984
1983

The 1983-94 figures represent what was actually spent, not the allotted operating budget for the fiscal year.

** *The 1995 figure is the amount budgeted.*

Source: U.S. Department of Commerce and International Trade Reporter

shipment values that they have only a marginal effect on the nation's trade figures.

FEDERAL POLICY: RHETORIC VS. REALITY

Given this record, and given more than a decade of government and business community discussion about "global competitiveness," it might have been reasonable in recent years to expect a powerful federal government commitment to improving the nation's export performance.

Yet despite high-profile campaigns to secure the passage of GATT and, earlier, the North American Free Trade Agreement (NAFTA), that commitment has not materialized in the form of fresh resources.

While funding for the International Trade Administration of the U.S. Department of Commerce rose slightly during the 1980s, the additional funds were spent principally on investigations into unfair trade complaints. Support for the U.S. and Foreign Commercial Service, the nation's principal trade-promotion agency, stagnated throughout the decade. Market increases since 1993 have funded a few overseas posts, participation in defense conversion programs, and greater attention to big emerging markets. *(See Figure 2.)*

Consequently, staff vacancies go unfilled for long periods in the overseas offices of the world's greatest industrial power. And fax messages from U.S. businesses go unanswered near the end of the fiscal year, because our foreign posts have run out of money.

In fact, what the federal government spends on export promotion is, in relative terms, a mere fraction of what our major industrial competitors spend. In a 1992 study, the U.S. General Accounting Office found that the U.S. federal government spent only 59 cents on promotion for every $1,000 of nonagricultural exports, compared to $1.62 for the United Kingdom, $1.71 for Italy and $1.99 for France.[15] *(See Figure 3.)* The German government spent less—22 cents—but that's only because German export promotion is handled through massive investments by its chamber of commerce system.

Despite **the export underachievement of U.S. firms, the federal government spends only a fraction, in relative terms, of what our major industrial competitors spend on export promotion.**

Moreover, while our competitors are spending heavily to promote their highest-value exports, the United States has long spent most of its meager resources on its *lowest*-value export: agriculture. Although it represents only 10 percent of the value of U.S. exports, agriculture garners 75 percent of our federal export-promotion spending.

By contrast, manufactured products, which represent 82 percent of the value of U.S. exports, receive only 10 percent of federal export-promotion funding.[16] What money and technical support *are* available

FIGURE 3. **NONAGRICULTURAL EXPORT PROMOTION OUTLAYS: 1990**

SELECTED NATIONAL GOVERNMENTS

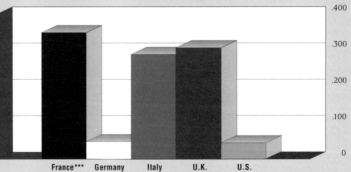

Outlays*
(Millions $

	France***	Germany	Italy	U.K.	U.S.

Outlays per
$1,000 exports

Outlays per
$1,000 GDP

* In all countries, except the United States, the spending includes estimates provided by government officials. Outlays do not include state and local government export-promotion spending and are only for "traditional" export-promotion activities such as awareness promotion, counseling, information, and trade event programs.

** Based on the following conversions using 1990 average exchange rates per U.S. dollar: France— 5.7 francs; Germany— 1.7 deutsche marks; Italy— 1254.3 lire; United Kingdom— 0.59 pounds sterling.

*** In all countries except France, this spending does not include money spent on agricultural promotion. French officials were unable to separate the agricultural spending from the total but told us that most of this spending is on nonagricultural programs.

Sources: GAO analysis of funding information provided by government officials.
Organization for Economic Cooperation and Development (OECD) Main Economic Indicators for
Gross Domestic Product and Monthly Statistics of Foreign Trade.

for manufactured export development typically go to large corporations—firms whose combined percentage of total exports has been essentially flat for years.[17] Until recently, service exports such as tourism, engineering and construction—worth an estimated $32 billion—have received little attention from trade development programs.

Recently, the federal government has attempted to "rationalize" its export promotion programs. The first National Export Strategy, mandated by the Export Enhancement Act of 1992 and published in September 1993, proposed restructuring a number of federal export-promotion programs. But the real resources have changed little. However strongly the administration and Congress may stress the importance of international trade, there is no evidence that either is willing to back up the rhetoric with increased federal financial support for export promotion.

State governments began taking global competition seriously more than a decade ago. But the explosion of state budget deficits in the recession years of the early 1990s sharply curtailed how much state governments could do.

STATE GOVERNMENT STEPS IN

Faced with recessions, industrial restructuring and federal budget cuts, state governments began taking global competition seriously more than a decade ago. State international trade agencies began growing in earnest in the early 1980s. Between 1984 and 1990, state international budgets grew at an average annual rate of 40 percent. By 1990, total state spending on international trade development totaled more than $90 million, roughly half of what the U.S. Department of Commerce was spending on international trade promotion and development.

But the explosion of state budget deficits in the recession years of the early 1990s sharply slowed this growth. While state international budgets increased slightly overall, many saw cutbacks—though often less severe than in other state programs. *(See Figure 4.)* In 1992, states were spending an average of only one penny on international trade development per $100 of manufactured exports—even as they, like the federal government, stressed the importance of global competitiveness. *(See Figure 5.)*

FIGURE 4. STATE INTERNATIONAL APPROPRIATIONS: 1984-92*

(THOUSANDS OF DOLLARS)

STATE	FY92	FY90	FY88	FY86	FY84
Alabama	1,085	1,105	1,330	600	600
Alaska	1,397	3,448	1,500	790	N/A
Arizona	950	700	342	478	200
Arkansas	862	697	500	500	400
California	8,260	10,556	10,450	5,700	460
Colorado	1,057	1,008	700	220	150
Connecticut	995	476	800	625	350
Delaware	940	441	241	75	N/A
Florida	3,500	2,900	2,300	1,587	725
Georgia	2,885	3,362	1,913	1,296	904
Hawaii	9,827	8,650	287	225	200
Idaho	622	242	160	25	35
Illinois	6,600	N/A	2,900	2,632	2,500
Indiana	3,000	1,884	1,076	676	560
Iowa	1,493	1,900	1,400	500	370
Kansas	N/A	N/A	500	132	82
Kentucky	N/A	1,075	1,100	N/A	838
Louisiana	850	1,675	471	300	N/A
Maine	N/A	390	150	N/A	N/A
Maryland	4,318	5,000	1,900	1,400	N/A
Massachusetts	1,015	625	836	438	100
Michigan	3,400	5,072	2,275	1,967	1,481
Minnesota	N/A	N/A	1,900	2,202	N/A
Mississippi	1,500	1,800	500	400	N/A
Missouri	2,092	1,800	1,100	900	580
Montana	567	561	100	86	68
Nebraska	168	168	N/A	N/A	275

22

Nevada	380	400	298	160	N/A
New Hampshire	N/A	90	7	N/A	7
New Jersey	1,844	2,400	4,718	1,600	635
New Mexico	337	238	144	N/A	7
New York	5,082	5,300	3,300	3,040	2,500
North Carolina	2,000	N/A	1,600	950	950
North Dakota	470	211	N/A	N/A	80
Ohio	3,107	3,500	2,800	2,500	1,900
Oklahoma	2,192	1,730	1,250	N/A	500
Oregon	3,300	5,531	2,260	739	530
Pennsylvania	900	1,200	820	845	N/A
Rhode Island	240	N/A	295	275	326
South Carolina	1,707	1,649	595	N/A	376
South Dakota	387	190	51	51	N/A
Tennessee	651	568	304	575	575
Texas	2,714	3,296	398	253	308
Utah	1,100	1,000	1,055	550	120
Vermont	180	200	18	N/A	N/A
Virginia	3,036	3,100	1,500	900	900
Washington	4,600	1,900	1,940	1,940	N/A
West Virginia	375	400	N/A	N/A	N/A
Wisconsin	4,464	2,358	1,300	725	535
Wyoming	329	310	300	355	N/A
Total	**$96,779**	**$91,107**	**$61,683**	**$39,211**	**$21,245**
Average**	**$2,151**	**$2,025**	**$1,312**	**$980**	**$590**

Figures include budget for export promotion, investment recruitment and, in some cases, ports, agriculture and tourism. They do not reflect state allocations to nonprofit organizations for purposes of trade development.

** *Averages do not include states with "N/A" for that year.*

Source: NASDA 1992 State Export Program Database

23

FIGURE 5. STATE TRADE OFFICE BUDGETS: 1992

(SELECTED MEASURES)

STATE	PER CAPITA*	PER PRODUCTION WORKER	PER $100 OF MFT'D EXPORTS
Alabama	.07	1.08	.007
Alaska	1.65	78.96	.024
Arizona	.26	10.28	.014
Arkansas	.07	.97	.011
California	.22	5.63	.009
Colorado	.32	10.72	.035
Connecticut	.16	3.04	.009
Delaware	.47	11.11	.017
Florida	.14	6.13	.009
Georgia	.14	2.43	.010
Hawaii	.63	60.70	.220
Idaho	.35	7.99	.031
Illinois	.36	6.96	.023
Indiana	.32	4.34	.026
Iowa	.43	7.81	.043
Kansas	.57	11.32	.051
Kentucky	N/A	N/A	N/A
Louisiana	.09	3.17	.002
Maine	N/A	N/A	N/A
Maryland	.40	16.98	.039
Massachusetts	.16	3.46	.008
Michigan	.07	1.21	.003
Minnesota	.49	9.80	.030
Mississippi	.10	1.32	.012
Missouri	.34	6.78	.043
Montana	.19	10.42	.051

Nebraska	.04	.80	.004
Nevada	.16	11.24	.035
New Hampshire	N/A	N/A	N/A
New Jersey	.09	2.33	.006
New Mexico	.22	12.34	.089
New York	.21	6.34	.013
North Carolina	N/A	N/A	N/A
North Dakota	.16	9.13	.027
Ohio	.21	3.34	.012
Oklahoma	.43	12.25	.060
Oregon	.70	13.79	.035
Pennsylvania	.01	.16	.001
Rhode Island	.08	1.28	.008
South Carolina	.03	.44	.002
South Dakota	.30	9.33	.083
Tennessee	.05	.67	.004
Texas	.09	2.79	.003
Utah	.35	9.43	.021
Vermont	.16	3.19	.003
Virginia	.18	3.82	.010
Washington	.58	14.15	.009
West Virginia	.04	1.36	.004
Wisconsin	.03	.42	.002
Wyoming	N/A	N/A	N/A
U.S. Average	**.21**	**4.63**	**.011**

* Based on 1990 Census Figures

Sources: 1992 NASDA Exporter Data Base, 1991 Survey of Manufacturers, U.S. Department of Commerce

THE INTERNATIONAL STATE: CRAFTING A STATEWIDE TRADE DEVELOPMENT SYSTEM

YESTERDAY'S EXPORTING: ECONOMIC OPPORTUNITY

Exports mean economic growth. Exports also mean jobs— and better-paying jobs than nonexport work.

FOR THE NATION: JOBS AND ECONOMIC GROWTH. Exports mean economic growth. Though the nation's persistent trade deficits with Japan continue to capture the headlines, U.S. exports doubled between 1980 and 1990 and represented an increasingly important source of real economic growth. Indeed, even though relatively few U.S. firms export, and even though their exports accounted for only an average of one-tenth of U.S. output between 1985 and 1994, those same exports were responsible for almost one-third of real U.S. economic growth.[18]

Exports also mean jobs. The Office of the U.S. Trade Representative estimates that each $1 billion in exports creates between

HOW JOB CREATION ESTIMATES CAN BE DERIVED

Attributing jobs to export sales is difficult. Employers themselves generally do not think in terms of which jobs on the factory floor are attributable to their exports. Since exports are typically only a small proportion of total sales, it can be hard to pinpoint who, besides the export manager (assuming there is one), relies on exports for his job. Nonetheless, it is inescapable that exports do create real jobs. Here is one quite conservative back-of-the-envelope methodology:

The domestic industry average for direct labor as a percent of sales, according to a 1995 survey by the National Association of Manufacturers, is 18 percent.[19] Eighteen percent of one billion dollars in export sales creates total wages of $180 million. If one uses the 1989 average hourly manufacturing wage of $10 per hour, or $20,800 per year, total export wages support 8,654 direct jobs. Using an extremely conservative multiplier of one indirect job stimulated by each direct manufacturing job, that $1 billion in exports creates some 17,300 jobs in all—and probably many more.

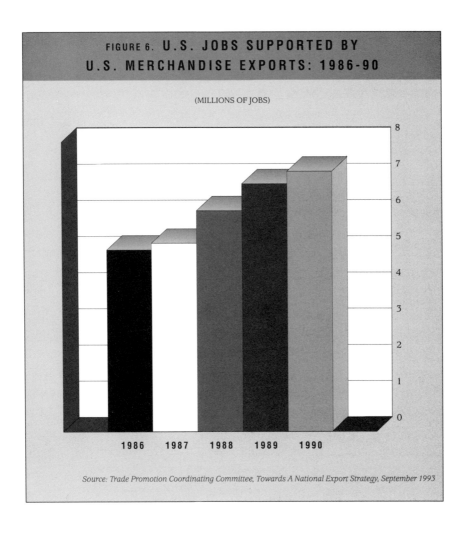

FIGURE 6. U.S. JOBS SUPPORTED BY U.S. MERCHANDISE EXPORTS: 1986-90

(MILLIONS OF JOBS)

1986 1987 1988 1989 1990

Source: Trade Promotion Coordinating Committee, Towards A National Export Strategy, September 1993

15,000 and 19,000 jobs, depending upon different assumptions about technology utilization, and wages and multipliers.[20] In all, current exports support some 7.2 million jobs in the United States.[21] *(See Figure 6.)* In 1990, in manufacturing alone, one in six U.S. jobs was supported directly or indirectly (as suppliers or subcontractors to the final producer) by exports.[22]

And these jobs pay better than nonexport jobs—almost 17 percent better, or about $3,400 more per year.[23] Indeed, during the 1980s, the U.S. Department of Labor analyzed the employment and earnings profiles of import-sensitive and export-sensitive industries in the United States. It defined "export-sensitive" as the 50 industries (at the four-digit SIC code level) that sell the highest proportion of total domestic production into export markets, while "import-sensitive" industries are the 50 in

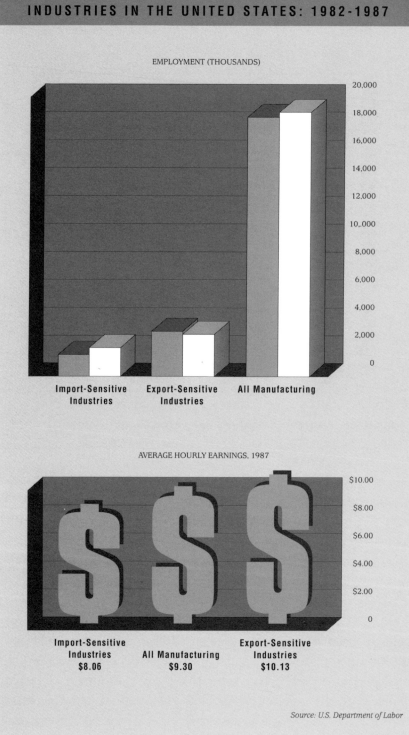

FIGURE 7. TRADE-SENSITIVE MANUFACTURING INDUSTRIES IN THE UNITED STATES: 1982-1987

EMPLOYMENT (THOUSANDS)

1982
1987

20,000
18,000
16,000
14,000
12,000
10,.000
8,000
6,000
4,000
2,000
0

Import-Sensitive
Industries

Export-Sensitive
Industries

All Manufacturing

AVERAGE HOURLY EARNINGS, 1987

$10.00
$8.00
$6.00
$4.00
$2.00
0

Import-Sensitive
Industries
$8.06

All Manufacturing
$9.30

Export-Sensitive
Industries
$10.13

Source: U.S. Department of Labor

which the highest proportion of our total domestic consumption comes from imports. *(See Figure 7.)* Not surprisingly, the study found that import-sensitive firms paid lower wages than manufacturing firms in general, while export-sensitive firms paid much higher wages.

One additional interesting point about U.S. exporting is often overlooked: Overseas affiliates of U.S. corporations are by far the largest importers of U.S. goods; that is, they are our largest export market.[24] This fact suggests that those who fear or oppose overseas investment— either by U.S. firms locating facilities elsewhere or by foreign firms locating here—as a threat to U.S. jobs and economic growth might more closely examine who gains and who loses in these deals.

FOR FIRMS: MARKETS, VIABILITY AND COMPETITIVE EDGE. While trade strengthens the national economy, its benefits for individual firms are perhaps more profound. Exporting creates new sources of profits and company growth, diversifies the customer base and thus decreases business cycle vulnerability, increases production economies of scale, and extends product life cycles by creating opportunities to sell to more markets over a longer period of time than is possible domestically. In addition, a study by the Institute for International Economics and the Manufacturing Institute has found that firms—both small and large—that export:

While trade strengthens the national economy, its benefits for individual firms are perhaps more profound—new sources of profits and growth, a diversified customer base, increased economies of scale, and extended product life.

- have worker productivity rates 30 to 50 percent higher than non-exporters

- have higher rates of innovation, with exporters adopting new technologies far more frequently and intensely than nonexporters

- fail one-third less frequently than nonexporters and shrink less than nonexporters during recessionary cycles

- have annual growth rates three to eleven percent higher than non-exporters

29

■ have a consistently higher level of employment growth[25]

What's more, the study found that, "Benefits from export reliance are widespread. They are not captured by a narrow set of corporate elites, but touch everyone...Though exports (and imports) can expose workers, firms and communities to unique costs and risks, the new evidence suggests that their widely shared benefits and opportunities are more than adequate to compensate."

> **C**ompanies that trade have access to market intelligence on competitors, customer trends and product standards that their nontrading neighbors don't— intelligence that can keep them ahead of the curve.

And there are even more compelling reasons to encourage trade by firms, especially the small and medium-sized firms that form the backbone of any economy. Companies that trade have access to market intelligence on competitors, customer trends and product standards that their nontrading neighbors don't—intelligence that can keep them ahead of the curve. Companies that trade are also exposed to new ideas and technologies used by customers, joint venture partners and even competitors. Therefore, they better understand the importance and rewards of modernization, and are more likely to make appropriate investments. Finally, companies that trade are exposed to potential partners with whom they can pool product lines and generate entirely new products, tapping new markets in the process.

TRADE TODAY: ECONOMIC IMPERATIVE

The harsh fact of contemporary economic life is that while firms may opt not to export, they cannot opt to avoid international competition. As industrial competitiveness expert Niels Christian Nielsen, managing director of the Danish Technology Institute, has noted, "The U.S. can no longer rely on its home market, because its home market is now an export market for everyone else."[26]

Indeed, it is almost impossible to identify a product or service that does *not* face international competition. Fresh-cut flowers are flown in daily from Columbia to cities throughout the nation, even as cast-iron manhole covers arrive on our shores from India. Insurance claims are

processed in Ireland. Even tourism and education service providers face
international competition.

LOWER COSTS, HIGHER TECHNOLOGY. The trends transforming international competition are continuing and irreversible; companies and
state economic development policymakers ignore them
at their peril. The decreasing costs of transportation, the
ease of global business communication, and the increasing availability and use of advanced technology in
production mean that new competitors—from Chile to
China—can, and do, challenge established U.S. industry
leaders. Technology tends to raise the value-added component of a product's final price, and the higher the value
added, the lower the transportation cost as a percentage
of total value. The net result is that, if the quality is high
enough, almost anyone can produce almost anything
and ship it almost anywhere.

DEMANDING CUSTOMERS, COMMANDING NICHES. In
addition, mass markets are shattering into global niche
markets. When a company produces a highly specialized
niche product—for example, a specialty medical device—
the domestic share of any one market is so narrow that
the company can grow only by selling globally within its
niche. Finding additional customers for such products—
wherever they are in the world—becomes crucial to
achieving sufficient production economies for firms to make a profit.
Moreover, niche markets emerge and mutate quickly, making access to
market intelligence crucial to company survival.

> **T**he trends
> transforming international
> competition—decreasing
> transportation costs, eased
> global communication, and
> increasingly advanced
> production technology—are
> continuing and irreversible.
> Companies and policymakers
> ignore them at their peril.

UNTAPPED POTENTIAL: THE DEVELOPMENT TASK

If the central purpose of economic development is to improve the standard and quality of living for citizens, then the challenges for economic
development policymakers may be to:

■■ encourage low-paying, low-productivity industries to move into
globally competitive niches, perhaps by blending trade development

assistance with help in strategic planning, industrial modernization and financial restructuring

■■ identify and aid the growing breed of "born-to-export" companies, many of which are quite small high-technology and service companies that do not conform to the norm of needing a long domestic track record before breaking into foreign markets

■■ help existing exporters to export more often, move into new markets and develop new products for export

If the key goal of economic development is to improve the standard and quality of living for citizens, one strategy of economic development policymakers must be to nurture export capabilities.

And there *is* enormous room for growth. Recent research by both The Urban Institute and The Pennsylvania State University suggests that many states with industries that produce products with identifiable overseas demand are performing well below their potential.[27]

Even very small, incremental improvements can have enormous effects. After a detailed analysis of existing export data, Leslie Stroh, editor and publisher of *The Exporter* magazine, discovered that, "If every exporter increased its export business by just one average-sized shipment per month, U.S. exports would grow by $40 billion in a year."[28] The impact of new shipments from *new* exporters would be even more dramatic.

Rural America: A Trade Development Challenge

If most American firms are behind the competitive curve in trade, rural firms are more so. Rural America may export tremendous quantities of agricultural and other commodities, but this has not "internationalized" its communities and businesses. In communities where commodity production has been the principal economic activity for generations— where, in the past, "marketing" simply meant getting the grain to the grain elevator—businesses and individuals have little or no exposure to the increasingly essential process of tracking, researching, anticipating and penetrating distinct and distant consumer markets. Nor are they fully aware of the growing need to pursue those markets by developing new and ever-changing products.

Although rural America today is far more dependent upon manufacturing than agriculture for jobs, it has little experience with, or even access to, nonagricultural U.S. export-development programs. And yet rural firms and communities *must* shatter their international isolation if they are to survive.

SITUATION: DEVELOPMENT DISADVANTAGES

The historic development disadvantages of rural economies that tend to reinforce such isolation are well-documented:

■■ *The distance penalty.* Because of their physical distance and social isolation from urban areas, rural citizens, businesses and organizations may have difficulty obtaining critical information.

■■ *Lack of scale economies.* Rural firms often do not produce enough volume to achieve what economists call "economies of scale." Likewise, they have fewer local firms to partner with to produce new products and reach new markets, or to trade ideas and compete with as a spur to innovation.

■■ *Underdeveloped infrastructure.* Rural areas often lag behind urban places in the quantity or quality of traditional infrastructure, such as roads, water and sewer, as well as telecommunications and technology.[29]

Other, less obvious barriers are even more formidable:

■■ *Lack of industrial diversity.* Rural economies often are narrowly based, dependent on a sole commodity-grade natural resource industry or low-wage branch manufacturing plant, neither of which is particularly responsive to local influence.

> **I**f most American firms are behind the competitive curve in trade, rural firms are more so. And yet rural firms and communities must shatter their international isolation if they are to survive.

■■ *Complacency and lack of market knowledge.* Many rural leaders and their constituents are unaware of how rural America's role is changing in the global economy. Far too often, they understand little about markets and tend to rely on outdated economic development methods.

As Tom Bonnett, an analyst for the Council of Governors' Policy Advisors, notes: "Rural communities are increasingly competing for jobs and incomes with all other locations throughout the world... most rural communities are not fundamentally in competition with urban America, nor are they competing among themselves to foster greater business and employment opportunities as the national economy is restructured."[30]

■■ *Limited demand for and supply of development resources.* Because the commodities they produce are "marketed" by international commodity brokers, there is little demand for market development assistance in rural areas. Consequently, private sector capacity to provide such services, or simply even to offer knowing advice, tends to be in short supply. Likewise, the provision of public trade development services for rural manufacturers is scarce compared to what is available to their urban counterparts.

> **F**ar too often, rural leaders understand little about markets and tend to rely on outdated economic development methods.

Moreover, the bulk of public funding available for rural economic development programs still originates in the U.S. Department of Agriculture and is focused narrowly on farming and forestry issues, while the bulk of fresh development thinking originates in state or private nonprofit organizations that tend to have limited knowledge of rural needs. For example, many state economic development initiatives emphasize high-growth, high-technology sectors that seldom exist in rural areas.

Typically, such initiatives also are poorly funded and thus less likely to reach widely dispersed rural firms. Indeed, few state economic development programs have explicit rural outreach components. A 1994 phone survey of predominantly rural states west of the

Mississippi River revealed that only two states, Minnesota and Washington, had an international trade development program with an explicit strategy for reaching rural businesses.[31]

- ■■ *Limited local capacity.* Even where development programs do exist, firms in rural communities often have no mechanism for learning about, much less accessing, available assistance. And few rural communities have the professional capacity needed to make sense out of disparate, poorly integrated state and federal development resources.

SOLUTION: TOWARDS A TRADING SYSTEM

A restructured system of state, regional and local trade programs could do much more to make professional services accessible to *all* firms and communities prepared to compete globally.

But *should* states create special rural trade development initiatives, separate from mainstream programs? Almost certainly not: the fiscal and human resources available for economic development, rural or otherwise, are far too limited to be further divided. Moreover, such programs would serve only to reinforce a false dichotomy between rural and urban economies, rather than forge them into coherent, integrated statewide or substate regional economies.

Yet, in the years ahead, access to economic and political power may be denied to those without knowledge of, if not experience in, the global trading system. It is clear, then, that rural economic separatism—and neglect—must end. As subsequent chapters will show, a *restructured system* of state, regional and local trade programs could do much more to make professional services accessible not simply to rural firms and communities, but to *all* firms and communities prepared to compete globally.

Trade, especially exporting, is a public obsession in most industrial nations and in many newly developing ones. Throughout Europe, for example, government and industry, often with the active participation of labor, work together to devise comprehensive trade development strategies backed by sophisticated—and, often, jointly operated—trade assistance services. Both the public and private sectors make significant investments in delivering high-value, individually customized trade-assistance services to firms, focusing special attention on smaller firms.[32]

Trade Assistance in the U.S.: Programs in Search of a System

As the importance of industrial competitiveness has grown over the past decade, U.S. states, substate regional organizations, nonprofits and industry groups have gradually crafted economic development strategies that incorporate the requisites of competitiveness. They have worked to deliver modern industrial technologies to small and medium-sized firms. They have designed new vehicles for accessing investment capital, new education reforms and new workforce training systems. They have invested in the infrastructure of the new economy—information, transportation and communication.

U.S. states, substate regional organizations, nonprofits and industry groups have all focused their attention on competitiveness-building initiatives—but have little to show for their efforts.

NO MARKET PLAN

In the public sector, such economic development initiatives are not unlike the investments a private firm might make in new equipment, worker training and product design. States typically point to "increased competitiveness" as the hoped-for outcome of these development initiatives, but that's a little like a firm saying its goal is "increased sales" without spelling out how many sales or how those sales will be achieved. In fact, no reputable business makes such investments without a market plan—that is, without a strategy for reaching its customers in its target markets with new or improved products.

States, too, need market plans for their economic development programs. A state that develops a world-class industrial modernization program and a world-class workforce development program is, for all intents and purposes, "all dressed up with nowhere to go" if it does not also have a world-class trade assistance *system* to connect its firms with global markets.

In today's truly global economy, *a state's trade assistance system is the market plan for its economic development strategy*. No market plan, no sales growth. No sales growth, no business growth. No business growth, no employment and income growth.

PRIORITY: LOW AND LANGUISHING

A state's trade assistance system is its market plan. No market plan, no sales or business growth. No business growth, no employment and income growth. And the United States has no such system.

But the United States has no such system. At the federal level, decades of inattention have produced a disparate array of poorly funded programs scattered among some 19 agencies. Perhaps worse, they have yielded little research on the export behavior or assistance needs of small and medium-sized firms, even less evaluation of existing services, and scanty, virtually unusable state-level census trade data.[33]

At the state level, although many states have struggled to fill the export assistance gaps, they are hobbled by an array of political and fiscal difficulties. Governors and legislators propose initiatives that purport to advance economic growth and global competitiveness, but trade development usually gets upstaged by more visible, local crises. Both political and budget support languish.

Within the private sector, only a handful of national trade associations operate international programs, and even fewer provide concrete market-development services for their members. Some local chambers of commerce have international trade committees but, once again, almost none provide direct services to members. Indeed, the national U.S. Chamber of Commerce has struggled for years to support an extremely modest international division.

And, at the level of individual business, it is perhaps not surprising that American industries are not inclined to think about exporting, given the uneven and lackluster interest of their own industry associations. The National Federation of Independent Business (NFIB) regularly polls its members about the importance of 75 business issues. Exporting consistently ranks dead last; even import competition rattles around at the bottom of the list. The NFIB's conclusion: Exporting isn't a problem because its member companies, for the most part, don't export much.[34]

State Trade Efforts: Struggling to Make Do

From the point of view of a state trade director, legislative and gubernatorial disinterest in trade efforts may actually be preferable to some of the attention they *do* receive. Governors, eager to demonstrate global economic consciousness, often schedule overseas trade missions that absorb enormous amounts of staff time and energy from the state development agency. The entire effort may be negated by cynical media, which tend to label every trade mission, no matter how important the market or how grueling the schedule, a "junket."

State trade offices typically cycle between two equally difficult operating conditions: ever-expanding demands and on-again/off-again support.

Indeed, state trade offices typically cycle between two equally difficult operating conditions: ever-expanding demands and on-again/off-again support. The handicaps under which these programs must struggle, detailed below, are many.

OVERWORKED, UNDERFED

Being a state trade director is hardly an enviable position. Governors and legislators establish new trade programs or services, often for no better

Most state trade offices attempt to offer training, counseling, leads, trade fair aid, trade missions, catalogue show participation, overseas offices and foreign investment recruitment—without the resources to support these services.

reason than that a neighboring state has done so. But seldom do they provide the funding necessary to ensure that these services are delivered professionally and to enough clients to make a measurable difference. Indeed, the range of products and services offered by most state trade offices, when compared with these offices' staffing and budget resources, illustrates a wide gap between ambition (or mandates) and actual capacity.[35]

Despite widely differing economic histories, current economic conditions and budgets, most state trade offices offer, or attempt to offer, roughly the same broad menu of services: training, counseling, trade leads, trade fair assistance, trade missions, catalogue show participation, overseas offices and foreign investment recruitment, among others.[36] Historically, the largest state trade program expenditures support overseas offices and trade missions, which often have poorly defined objectives and may or may not yield results commensurate with potential, in part because few offices have the resources to follow up with participating firms. Thus, even though state trade agencies may offer many other services, few resources are actually available to support them.

To compound this problem, few trade offices are able to hire the seasoned export-market development specialists that businesses need to shepherd them through their first overseas sales. Restrictive state personnel rules and budgets too small to support professional salaries mean that many trade agencies, thinly staffed to begin with, are operated by workers who are young and relatively inexperienced—albeit hard-working, dedicated and enthusiastic. In addition, frequent personnel turnover frustrates institutional learning and capacity-building; at the same time, it impairs credibility with business clients and overseas contacts.

Event-driven, not strategy-driven

State trade offices tend to be event-driven, rather than strategy-driven. In part, this is based on tradition. Events such as trade shows, trade missions, seminars and visiting delegations have long been the principal activities of trade offices. Consequently, state trade staff tend to be in a constant state of event-preparation, with relatively little time or incentive to consider the results or to develop the kind of deep, long-term relationships with their clients that are the key to successful export growth. *(For an exception, see Oregon's Approach: Sales, Not Promotion.)*

This problem is exacerbated by political pressure. High-level elected and appointed officials want to conduct high-visibility trade activities that demonstrate that the state is busily engaged in international economic development. But this focus on *activities* tends to ignore the question of what real businesses actually *need*. Few state trade programs have undertaken a thorough analysis of client needs, relying instead on assumptions about business needs.

OREGON'S APPROACH: SALES, NOT PROMOTION

"Promotion is a waste of money," says former International Trade Division director Glenn Ford. One of the basic questions that a governor has to address is, what is our fundamental goal in this international program? Is it to help a lot of tiny companies or is it to maximize employment and economic activity in the state?"[37]

While other state trade programs cover a broad range of promotional activities and try to address a wide range of issues for virtually any firm that walks in the door, Oregon's strategy has been disciplined and selective, focusing narrowly on finding overseas representation for the state's mid-market manufacturers and traded-service companies—those

with $2-20 million in sales per year.

"These firms don't need motivating, they need markets," Ford has said. "The more specialized their products are, the sooner their domestic markets get saturated and the sooner they need overseas markets."

Oregon was the first state to execute detailed contracts specifying how the state and the client company would jointly develop the internationalization strategy, explore markets and representation options, and negotiate agreements with overseas partners. "In effect," explained Ford, "we join their company and they join

(continued on next page)

ours." The state's client companies pay the travel expenses of state trade officers and, more recently, fees for specific services.

One of the great strengths of the Oregon program is that it knows precisely how its client firms fare—how much their international sales are worth, and the number of jobs retained or created—because the contract requires client firms to report these data to the trade division.

But there are weaknesses too. First, the state has only had the resources to provide this kind of direct, professional market-development assistance to 40-50 firms per year. Thus, no matter how successful the program has been, its total impact is limited. Linking the program more directly to the state's key industries program and its associated multifirm networks could substantially improve this scale problem, but that has yet to occur.

Second, as currently structured, the state is in direct and subsidized competition with private sector export-service providers for the same clientele.

Despite its market-driven, businesslike approach, these weaknesses—plus the usual upheavals of the election cycle—have placed the program in jeopardy. A new director is reviewing the program.

UNCERTAIN CLIENTELE

State trade programs typically are charged with increasing the export sales of small and medium-sized businesses. Beyond this rather broad mandate, they usually are unclear about who their target clients are, and they seldom have the time or resources to determine the specific needs of individual firms. Thus, under pressure to show quick results, trade offices end up focusing their efforts on firms that are well-prepared for or already experienced in exporting. As a result, smaller, export-willing but not-yet-ready firms that might have significant growth potential often go without assistance.

There is, of course, nothing inherently wrong with serving only the most likely to succeed, but that is seldom the expressed objective of state policy.

What's more, doing so places state trade offices in direct—and subsidized—competition with private export-service providers who, in search of profits, seek the same clients. (It almost goes without saying that larger, more experienced firms also are more willing and able to pay private providers for trade development services, which argues against a large public role in serving this segment.) Finally, such a strategy overlooks many new, small, high-value niche producers that, from the start, include export market development as an integral part of their business strategies.

It is true that, in general, smaller businesses are harder to reach, have limited capacity to plan an export strategy, and thus require more help from state trade staff. But they are an untapped and potentially rich target market for government trade services. A recent survey by Arthur Anderson's Enterprise Group and National Small Business United found that only 29 percent of firms surveyed felt they were in a "nonexport business," yet few of the remaining 71 percent exported.[38] Reacting to such data, the U.S. Department of Commerce has chosen to focus on the roughly 103,000 firms which its "Exporter Database" suggests are motivated but infrequent exporters—firms that export only sporadically, to few markets and at low shipment values. The Commerce Department's ability to provide direct technical assistance to individual firms, however, is even more limited than a state's.

Under pressure to show quick results, trade offices end up focusing their efforts on firms that are well-prepared for or already experienced in exporting.

BREADTH VS. DEPTH

Because, as mentioned earlier, their legislative and/or executive mandates often are vague and broad (not to mention underfunded), state trade programs often are wide and thin. Trade-lead systems, seminars and phone contacts yield impressive numbers of "firms assisted," but few states are capable of helping more than a few firms actually develop and close trade transactions. They don't have the time, the money or, in many cases, the skills to do so.

Not surprisingly, therefore, program directors struggle annually with the problem of producing well-supported assessments of their program

43

results. In addition, some state trade programs steer away from providing deal-specific assistance simply for fear of recriminations should the deal fail, or of complaints about unfair competition or favoritism from rival companies.

Overseas offices: high cost, uneven impact

After rising steadily throughout the 1980s, the number of state overseas trade offices peaked in 1990 at 163 and has since declined somewhat.[39] Typically the largest single cost center of state trade programs, the establishment of these offices has often been more politically than strategically driven. States have stampeded to open offices in "hot" locations whether they could afford them or not—and, more importantly, whether or not the location represented good market opportunities for the mix of firms in the state. Moreover, most cities in which state overseas offices are located already have a U.S. Foreign and Commercial Service office; fewer than a dozen state-covered cities lack one.

The establishment of overseas trade offices, typically the largest single cost center of state trade programs, has often been more politically than strategically driven.

These features cause state budget analysts to perennially question the state's presence abroad. The result, in the words of one recent study, is "a lack of consistent budget and personnel support which, in the worst cases, leads to a merry-go-round of office openings and closings."[40]

The same study often found fuzzy reasons for office locations. The largest number of offices in Europe, for example, was in Brussels, yet office managers there confessed that they had little contact with either the European Union or NATO—even though proximity to those organizations was the rationale for the offices' location. Moreover, overseas offices see few visitors either from the United States or from the country in which they are located—an average of only six visitors per month in the European study—suggesting that there may be little justification for high-overhead office suites.

Most important, however, the day-to-day purposes of these offices often are only vaguely defined, and their performance is rarely evaluated critically. Overseas offices can be and, in some instances, *are* high-performing components of a state trade system, but few have clear, measurable performance objectives. One exception, Idaho, recently held a competition to select its Asian representation, and executed performance contracts with winning entrants specifying explicit return-on-investment targets.

STRONG RIVALS, WEAK PARTNERSHIPS

In any state, there are many public, private and nonprofit organizations that purport to provide export services. These organizations should support each other's efforts but rarely do. The net result is service fragmentation, dilution of public and private resources and limited real impact on the trade behavior of firms.

In state government alone, for example, both the economic development and agriculture departments typically have trade promotion programs, but they seldom interact. Politics works to keep them both in business, since trade promotion provides opportunities for agency heads (many of whom are elected) to appear in public doing something positive. Yet the dilution of limited state funds into two departments' programs often means the state will have two weak programs, rather than one strong one.

> **T**he many public, private and nonprofit organizations that purport to provide export services in each state should support each other's efforts— but rarely do.

Outside state government, there are many more trade development rivals: federal agencies, universities, trade associations, chambers of commerce, port authorities, world trade centers, export clubs and private export consultants, to name but a few. Most states have some kind of coordinating or partnership mechanism (such as a governor's advisory board) with at least some of these other would-be service providers, but few of these partnerships actually share and sustain responsibility for strategy development, program design, service delivery or evaluation. Likewise, federally appointed District Export Councils (DECs) may serve as a springboard to deeper public-private partnerships, but DECs have neither the mandate nor the independent authority to affect state or federal budgets, programs or policies—much less nonprofit, university or private export-service providers.

Most often, advisory boards composed of state, federal and nonprofit organizations meet infrequently and tend to be forums for staff briefings, rather than brisk discussion of strategies and tactics. Moreover, their members seldom have a vested interest in the partnership's success. Private corporations occasionally serve as event co-sponsors or even passive donors, but seldom are they active partners.

State Trade Results: Significant Return, Limited Impact

Despite all the preceding obstacles—even though they are chronically underfunded and understaffed, buffeted by the political whims of both the executive and legislative branches of government, and stuck on a treadmill of routine activities of uncertain effectiveness—state trade offices appear to have considerable potential. Inefficiency, after all, does not preclude significant returns. Ironically, trade offices may be among the most effective generators of real economic development—measured in business sales—per dollar of public expenditure in government.

Some studies show that state trade offices are among the most effective generators of real economic development— measured in business sales— per dollar of public expenditure in government.

HIGH RETURN ON INVESTMENT?

Little empirical research has been done on the actual return on investment (in terms of business sales and tax revenue) of export assistance programs, and few states have attempted to assess the extent of this return. But the information that is available is intriguing.

One recent study found that each additional $1,000 spent on export promotion can generate $423,000 in export sales growth.[41] The return on investment of state export-finance programs, which are closer to the point of final sale than, say, export training initiatives, is easier to track. The Export Assistance Center of Washington, which arranges financing for very small export deals, reports a $9.00

return for each dollar spent.[42] At one point, California estimated that its export finance program returns $300 for each dollar invested.[43]

A COVERAGE/IMPACT TRADE-OFF

Although these figures are encouraging, and show that state export-assistance programs may be effective with the firms that they reach, the plain fact is that their impact on the export behavior of the state's firms *overall* may be almost negligible. The reason has to do with the trade-off that such programs face between providing broad and shallow versus deep and narrow assistance to the state's firms.

> **B**ut because of the trade-offs that state trade offices face between broad and shallow versus deep and narrow assistance, their *overall* impact may be negligible.

On the one hand, providing data, referrals and contacts costs relatively little and is an essential and classic task of government. But moving beyond providing information is difficult and raises a central strategic question: Should state trade offices aim for maximum exposure or maximum impact? Going for exposure gets the word out, but it doesn't get deals made. Going for impact gets deals made, but no state trade office has the resources to provide the kind of in-depth assistance that yields deals for more than a few dozen individual firms in a given year.

SERVICE USAGE AND VALUE: MIXED MESSAGE

A recent survey of small and medium-sized exporting manufacturers, conducted by The Kenan Institute of Private Enterprise at the University of North Carolina, sheds some light on these choices.[44] Kenan researchers found that:

- Only 15 percent of exporters use government market-information services, seminars and basic counseling services. State trade programs are the source of only 12-14 percent of this basic information assistance.

- State programs reach a little more than 20 percent of both small and medium-sized exporters. The U.S. Department of Commerce provides assistance to about 30 percent of small exporters and more than 40 percent of medium-sized exporters.

- Only about one-third of all exporters make use of the ten most commonly used trade services from any organized source (public, private, nonprofit).

- Of those who *did* use a service, 60 to 80 percent said it had an impact. With few exceptions, however, private sector for-profit organizations and other private companies—*not* federal, state or nonprofit organizations—provided the services that firms rated as "valued." Indeed, state trade offices were the source of only 9 percent of the "valued" services received by the businesses surveyed.[45]

To succeed in improving firms' global competitiveness, states must find ways to make use of the full range of potential export-service providers— including private sector and for-profit firms.

- Perhaps not surprisingly, the more detailed and transaction-specific the service, the more likely that the valued services cited were those of private sector organizations rather than state programs.

Several clear messages emerge from this survey:

- There are many providers of export services, but relatively few users.

- Of those who do use export services, a sizable majority find them valuable, suggesting improved accessibility would be beneficial.

- None of the providers offers services that users value *across the board;* each is weak in some areas.

- If states are going to succeed in improving the global competitiveness of small and medium-sized firms, they must find ways to make use of the full range of potential export-service providers.

In short, as things now stand, effective trade services are too complex and sophisticated, the resources and skills required too limited, and the needs of firms too varied for state trade offices—or anyone else—to meet all of them *alone*. Moreover, as the next chapter will detail, the conditions of governance in the 1990s, and very likely well into the future, will not permit it.

CHAPTER 3. THE CHANGING STATE OF GOVERNANCE

Just as the world of private industry is restructuring, so too is the world of public policy and governance. The driving forces are the same: state trade offices must also adjust to new technology, expanding competition, budget austerity and consequent downsizing, and an increased focus on customers and the bottom line.

As a result, the terms and conditions of governance are changing. In the trade assistance field as in many others, new players are entering the picture, and old players are revising their roles and the services they offer. Gradually, a new set of rules is emerging.

New Conditions

Call it downsizing, rightsizing, rethinking, or reinventing, the fact is that how we think about the purpose and process of state economic development—and, within it, state trade-assistance programs—is changing rapidly.

When state budgets were flush and growing, it was easy for policymakers to overlook the limitations and outright failures of traditional bureaucratic program management, and to focus instead on increasing the number and size of programs. But the recession of the early 1980s, with its skyrocketing state budget deficits and Draconian program cuts, focused executive, legislative and public attention on performance as never before. Cumbersome administrative procedures, the inefficiencies and political shifts of two- and four-year election cycles, program fragmentation, and ambiguity about actual accomplishments generated widespread public distrust and persuaded the very clients of economic development programs that government programs did not "speak to the bottom line of business." Not

> **T**he recession of the early 1980s, with its skyrocketing state budget deficits and Draconian program cuts, focused executive, legislative and public attention on performance as never before.

THE INTERNATIONAL STATE: CRAFTING A STATEWIDE TRADE DEVELOPMENT SYSTEM

only did businesses come to mistrust government agencies, they mistrusted, or simply did not seek help from, private sector programs supported by public funds.[46]

Given these harsh realities, something had to give. Unfortunately— or perhaps fortunately—what gave out was public patience. If there is a silver lining in this cloud, it is that extreme fiscal distress has been a liberating condition. In response, states have launched a wide array of initiatives aimed at addressing three core problems that have plagued economic development programs for years: scale, fragmentation and accountability.

THE PROBLEM OF SCALE

Even at their height, state trade programs have been able to provide tangible assistance to only a tiny percentage of export-capable firms. Through conferences, seminars and phone consultations, trade offices may have "contact with" hundreds of firms. As noted earlier, however, their staff and financial resources are so limited that most can move only a few dozen firms to the point of actually consummating export deals. And while the sales (and thus the tax revenue) generated from these relatively few concrete successes may outweigh the cost of providing the assistance, the plain fact is that the impact on the state's economy is marginal.

> Even at their height, state trade programs have been able to provide tangible assistance to only a tiny percentage of export-capable firms.

This is not, of course, a problem limited to trade offices. The problem of achieving an adequate scale of impact is endemic throughout the field of economic development. A recent report produced by the Joint Legislative Committee on Trade and Economic Development of Oregon—a state with one of the most progressive economic development programs in the nation—underscores the problem:

> *As a state, Oregon has spent between $50 and $100 million per year on economic development in the past decade, trying to change the direction of an economy that has grown in total size to $55*

billion. *Measured in another way, Oregon's economy has more than 70,000 businesses with a payroll, and more than 7,000 firms in manufacturing alone. Yet in a given year, all the state's economic development programs may be able to reach only a small fraction of these businesses. A 1988 survey of small Oregon businesses showed that only 2 percent had any contact with the state's Economic Development Department.[47]*

Operating as they do in a kind of perpetual twilight of marginality, it is little wonder that the accomplishments of state economic development programs are unclear to the public at large, the business community, the legislature and even the programs' own department directors. And money is not necessarily the answer. Perhaps large increases in funding for trade and economic development would improve the scale of the impact, perhaps not. In any event, such increases are extremely unlikely anytime in the foreseeable future.

If state trade programs' problem of scale or marginality is to be solved, the solution will have to come from changing the way development is pursued, not from fresh funding.

In short, if the problem of scale or marginality is to be solved, the solution will have to come from changing the way development is pursued, not from fresh funding.

THE PROBLEM OF FRAGMENTATION

Until quite recently, few states (or cities, or counties) had strategic plans—business plans, in effect—for their economic development programs. Over the years, programs have been cobbled together, one initiative after another. Some are executive initiatives, others legislative mandates, still others federal requirements. The Oregon Joint Legislative Committee on Trade and Economic Development again:

In the past, Oregon, like many states, could be accused of the "merit badge" approach to economic development policy: each new innovation in economic development leads to the establishment of a separate new program, often unrelated to all other economic development activities.[48]

For the clients of these programs (and sometimes for the administrators as well), the result is an impenetrable maze. Businesses do not, as a general rule, turn to government when they have a problem. But those that do soon turn away again when they discover that there is no map of the maze, and that sometimes even the program administrators within it have no clear sense of the whole. While those clients who persist may, in the end, find someone or something capable of solving their problem, they are just as likely to find that the world of economic development programs has been organized to serve the convenience of bureaucracy, not customers.

At the very moment that businesses most need clarity, the trade assistance maze seems instead to spreading from the public sector to the private sector.

State trade programs typically are no less fragmented, with new ideas and services gradually being grafted onto an undernourished central core. For the would-be exporting firm, this fragmentation is compounded several-fold by the rapid proliferation of private sector, nonprofit and quasi-public organizations—port authorities, world trade centers, chambers of commerce, trade booster associations and so forth—in virtually every major metropolitan area in the nation. And as the decibel level of the global competitiveness debate increases, there are new entrants to the field every day. *(See "New Players" on page 56.)* At the very moment that businesses most need clarity, the trade assistance maze seems instead to be replicating itself in the private sector.

THE PROBLEM OF ACCOUNTABILITY

In state trade programs, as in other economic development programs, the annual or biennial legislative question—"What have you done with the funds we appropriated for you in the last budget?"—has been answered for years with "activity" numbers: the numbers of attendees at trade awareness seminars, numbers of phone or personal counseling sessions held, numbers of trade missions or trade fairs attended and the numbers of firms participating in them, numbers of leads listed in trade-lead databases, and the like. Only rarely is it answered with hard "outcome" figures on the actual export sales produced as a result of such state assistance.

Under current fiscal conditions, clinging to activity numbers while *hoping* for the best is no longer sufficient. Moreover, legislative audits of state trade programs have found that even these "results" are weakly documented, inaccurate and sometimes significantly exaggerated.[49] And even when results *are* expressed in terms of outcomes, these figures typically are not verified.

In part, this is because legislatures seldom ask for concrete results. More to the point, legislatures seldom seem seriously interested in results even when they are reported, since inputs like budgets and staff, rather than outcomes, are the traditional focus of legislative attention. Partly, too, it is because, in the absence of contractual agreements that stipulate sales reporting from client companies, it is often difficult to connect generalized trade assistance with completed export deals—that is, to connect cause with effect. Because of these difficulties, and because their limited resources are already spread too thin, few states have the ability to track accurately the results of the trade assistance they provide.

People who oversee the expenditure of public money have only sketchy information upon which to gauge the effectiveness of state trade-assistance programs.

Unfortunately, this disconnect has profound costs, both for those who govern and for the intended beneficiaries. The most obvious cost, and the one that has received the greatest attention given severe budget crises, is the absence of concrete information on accomplishments that can provide the feedback needed to improve services. People who oversee the expenditure of public money have only sketchy information upon which to gauge the effectiveness of state trade-assistance programs.

In the absence of real *outcome* data, the pressure to cut back or simply eliminate programs—programs that legislators acknowledge are important to the state's global competitiveness—is overwhelming, creating a condition of intolerable uncertainty. Conversely, for program managers, the absence of reliable outcome information makes it extremely difficult to claim credit and receive rewards for the progress they know they have helped effect. They must plead for support based on faith, not fact. That kind of support is in scant supply.

For the businesses that are the intended beneficiaries of state trade services, the disconnect between activity and outcome breeds skepticism, even cynicism. Businesses have a bottom line every day; government programs, they perceive, do not. Even in the case of trade assistance services, where the interaction between government and business is more direct than in many other economic development programs, businesses seldom acknowledge the assistance they receive and even more rarely credit that assistance for their success.

> **In the absence of real outcome data, the pressure to cut back or simply eliminate programs is overwhelming, creating a condition of intolerable uncertainty.**

In part, this is human nature. But it also is a reflection of the plain fact that businesses feel very little sense of ownership of these programs. With some notable exceptions, trade assistance services seldom are truly customized to the needs of individual firms. Typically, services are free or nearly so, and are offered on a take-it-or-leave-it basis. Under these circumstances, business community suspicion that "you get what you pay for" is perhaps understandable, if not entirely accurate. Thus, the irony is that the intended beneficiaries of state trade services feel neither loyal to them if they are well-served, nor aggrieved if they are not.

New Players

In Europe and elsewhere, trading has been so central to economic growth for so long that well-established relationships exist between public and private sector providers of various trade services. In the United States, by contrast, available services have tended to be fragmented and spotty.

Ten years ago, when state trade-assistance programs began to mushroom, they faced relatively few competitors: a disparate array of federal programs, a scattering of world trade centers, an occasional small-business development center with an international bent, and perhaps a handful of private-sector trade facilitators. Trade assistance services *still* are scattered among an array of public and private providers, and still too few direct working linkages exist among them.

As the importance and profitability of trade seeps into public consciousness, however, many more trade assistance providers are beginning to appear. Nonprofit organizations are venturing into the field. Individual entrepreneurs, some of them refugees from state trade offices, are entering the business of trade-relationship brokering. Law, accounting, financial and other firms are finding that offering trade development assistance is an imaginative way of attracting and retaining customers for other services. *(See Figure 8, next page.)*

THE FEDS REGROUP

Despite the fact that some seven million American jobs depend on exports, the nation has never had a clear set of objectives and strategies to guide its export promotion efforts. Programs have been scattered among some 19 federal agencies. In 1992, partly in response to a series of blistering critiques by the U.S. General Accounting Office, Congress enacted the Export Enhancement Act. Among other things, the legislation gave statutory standing to the federal Trade Promotion Coordinating Committee—previously an informal interagency body—and required it to produce a coherent strategy.

A more sensible strategy would have been for the federal government to focus its resources on the services that it alone can provide best—data collection, advocacy, overseas facilitation. State offices could then be one-stop shops for access to federal assistance.

The result, one year later, was the first annual National Export Strategy. Among other features, the strategy aims to coordinate export promotion policy, ensure better delivery of government export services to assist businesses, and provide a central source of information on export promotion services. The first National Export Strategy, which has since been updated, concentrated on improving the quality of overseas commercial functions, including advocacy before foreign governments, market research, and other duties performed by the U.S. Foreign and Commercial Service and commercial officers in U.S. embassies. In addition, the strategy gave priority to reducing licensing restrictions, promoting environmental and technology exports, and taking a proactive stance on international product standards. It also began the process of reorganizing and simplifying existing federal export-finance programs aimed at small businesses.

57

FIGURE 8. THE COLLAGE OF STAKEHOLDERS
IN A STATEWIDE TRADE SYSTEM

THE PRIVATE FOR-PROFIT SECTOR

Individual Client Businesses
Trade Service Consultants
Trade Intermediaries
Regional Corporations
- Utilities
- Banks
- Telecommunications

Industry Networks
Joint Venture Facilitators
Venture Capitalists
Business Incubators
Vendors
Suppliers

THE NONPROFIT SECTOR

State/Local Public Interest Groups
Foundations
World Trade Centers
Chambers of Commerce
NASDA
Manufacturing Technology Centers
"Think Tanks"
International Visitors Council
Sister Cities International
Industry Associations
Trade Associations

ACADEMIA

K-12 Schools
Colleges
International Programs of Universities
- Title VI
- CIBERs
- International Trade Centers
- "Think Tanks"
- Exchange Programs

Economic Development Programs Housed in Universities
- Industrial Extension
- Agricultural Extension
- SBDCs

NASBITE
Professors

OTHER STATE PROGRAMS

Investment Recruitment	Industrial Modernization
Defense Conversion	Minority Development
Transportation	Tourism
Rural Development	Agriculture
	Financing

LOCAL

Cities	Substate Regional Groups
Counties	
Civic Groups	Foreign Trade Zones
Ethnic Groups	

58

THE POPULAR MEDIA

Local and National Television

Local and National Radio

Local and National
Newspapers

Foreign Newspapers

Magazines

Trade Journals

GOVERNOR   ## LEGISLATURE

THE STATE TRADE OFFICE

STATE TRADE ADVISORS

- District Export Council
- State Rep. in Washington, D.C.
- "USTR Point of Contact"
- Individual Business Leaders
- Governor's Advisory Board

FOREIGN

Embassies/Trade Missions

Multilateral Development Banks

United Nations

Other Multilateral Organizations

Resident Aliens

Tourists

Students/Researchers

Business Visitors

THE FEDERAL GOVERNMENT

White House

Congress

General Accounting Office

Trade Promotion Coordinating
Committee (TPCC) Members

- Departments of:
  Commerce
  Agriculture
  Transportation
  Energy
  Education
  Labor
  State
  Treasury
  Defense
- Office of the U.S. Trade
  Representative
- U.S. Export-Import Bank
- Trade Development Agency
- Overseas Private Investment
  Corporation
- U.S. Agency for International
  Development
- Small Business Administration
- U.S. Environmental Protection
  Agency
- U.S. Information Agency
- Office of Management and Budget
- National Security Council
- National Economic Council
- Council of Economic Advisors

Other Federal Entities

- Peace Corps
- International Trade Commission
- Courts
- Congressional Research Service
- Commissions and Councils

On the issue of whether federal agencies should provide direct trade-assistance services to individual firms, the strategy is vague and sometimes flatly contradictory. It asserts, for instance, that the federal government will "wholesale" its export assistance to other service "retailers" closer to the customer. Yet at the same time, it announces the establishment of a large nationwide network of federal U.S. Export Assistance Centers (USEACs) that will retail federal programs directly to firms.

A more sensible strategy would have been for the federal government to focus its resources on the services that it alone can provide best and that its customers value most—for example, data collection, advocacy and overseas facilitation—and to make state offices one-stop shops for access to federal assistance, precluding the need for USEACs altogether.

CITIES GO GLOBAL

Increasingly, the leadership of cities—that is, the combined forces of city halls, chambers of commerce and other local organizations—is considering trade when designing economic development initiatives. Few cities have the resources to mount major initiatives on their own, so communities are pooling public, private and nonprofit resources. Some are even exploring regional trade-service delivery systems.

> Cities have tended to work independently of state trade offices. But resource scarcity may soon help both to recognize their shared goals and opportunities.

The National League of Cities has long promoted the need to "internationalize city hall," even among smaller communities.[50] In some larger cities, chambers of commerce have begun to move beyond their traditional social and political activities to explore how they might help deliver trade services to their members. Some have created full-time staff positions for international development.

Such initiatives have tended to be independent of state trade offices, with which city programs seldom communicate. But resource scarcity may soon help both to recognize their shared goals and opportunities.

POWER COMPANIES SEE THE LIGHT

Since gas and electrical utilities are in the business of selling power, they can grow only if their customers grow. In the past, power companies have been deeply involved in industrial recruitment. Even today, they are the principal advertisers in *Area Development* and *Site Selection* magazines, the best-known trade magazines that cater to recruiters and corporate-relocation specialists.

But the era of industrial relocation within the United States is on the wane. Even in its heyday, relatively few factories were wholly relocated, and their job-creation records were modest, especially compared to the number of new jobs created by existing businesses. And today, plant are far more likely to relocate to Southeast Asia or South America than to the American South, or anywhere else in the United States.

So, if power companies are to grow, they must find ways of helping their existing customers grow. Some are doing it by helping their customers enter international markets. *(See "Michigan State University: A Partnership With Power Companies.")*

If power companies are to grow, they must find ways of helping their existing customers grow. Some are doing it by helping their customers enter international markets.

It has not always been an easy sell, either internally or externally. Utility executives are naturally wary of partici-pating in an initiative with a distant impact on the bottom line. Moreover, existing nongovernmental export-service providers may resent a new-comer with so much clout.

These barriers notwithstanding, a joint venture with one or more utilities can bring state trade offices extraordinary assets for the task of trade development. Power and utility companies:

■■ have a *large sales force* that is in contact with businesses every day— something no state trade office could replicate

■■ are at the *junction of two networks*—industrial plant managers and economic development professionals

MICHIGAN STATE UNIVERSITY: A PARTNERSHIP WITH POWER COMPANIES

The International Business Development Center of Michigan State University (MSU) has long been a national leader in export development training. It created, and continues to refine, what is arguably the best software that firms and export service professionals can use to check companies for "export readiness."

Michigan-based Consumers Power Company (CP), convinced that it could, in effect, "export power" indirectly through the export successes of its customers, decided to assume some responsibility for its customers' export development. CP partnered with MSU to organize a 12- to18- month program, *Export Success*, to put CEOs on a fast track for trade.

The idea is to teach the basics of exporting through the closely supervised development of a real export plan tailored to the companies enrolled in the course. What is different about the MSU approach is its:

- goal of sustained exporting

- highly tailored business planning

- group education and training

- peer learning and mentoring plus long-term networking

- needs-based follow-up

- insistence on dealing with top management

- substantial client co-payment

In its first two years, CP selectively recruited and rigorously screened a handful of mid-sized companies that they identified as having the greatest export-growth potential—*and* the commitment to follow through. In 1993, nine firms "graduated" from the program; in 1994, six more joined them.

CP managed to keep expenses down by charging the firms a $4,800 fee and by collaborating with the experienced team at MSU. The effort involved an average of 25 percent of one CP manager's time, plus expenses for a limited amount of advice from a private trade-consulting company (Global Growth Associates), books and incidentals.

The program, although successful, went through changes as electric utilities hunkered down under the pressures of deregulation. With more than a dozen new exporters under its wing, CP decided to phase out its intensive involvement. Fortunately, gas utilities have fared better than electric utilities of late, and the MSU organizers have found an-other sponsor in the Michigan Consolidated Gas Company (MichCon). Consequently, two more classes of future exporters have begun the march into global markets through the program, now called *Great Exportations*.

- span local political jurisdictions and even state lines and, therefore, can help development officials envision programs that *serve functional economic regions*

- are more accustomed than government to *making long-term investments* and being patient about the outcomes

- are, as a result of deregulation and consequent competition, more *intent on customer service* than in the past

- are, in some instances, themselves *exporters* of power-generation equipment, consulting services and/or conservation services and technologies

> **A** joint venture with one or more utilities can bring state trade offices extraordinary assets for the task of trade development.

Though even power companies have limited resources, their service range is ambitious. *(See "Utility Companies: New Export Players.")* To help bring order to the industry's efforts, the Edison Electric Institute, in cooperation with the National Council for Urban Economic Development, has published both a guide to developing a utility-export program and a business guide to the exporting process.[51]

THE BANKS MAY FINANCE AGAIN

In virtually every major industrial nation in the world, the owner of a firm with an overseas order can walk around the corner to the local bank

A few utilities have been very active and creative in providing export services to their clients. Options run the full gamut of potential services—way beyond the predictable, one-time, event sponsorship. Most utilities are not "deep pockets," however, so few devote more than the full-time equivalent of a single staffer (some even less), and most specialize in just a few activities.

There is no discernable pattern in utilities' choices of activities, but the list below describes the wide range:

EXPORT LEADERSHIP

- serve on boards of local trade-service support organizations

- interact with local foreign-trade associations

- make contacts with foreign banks

- develop and/or own a world trade center

- serve as a "behind-the-scenes" player, to encourage the region to develop a trade service system

BASIC EXPORT EDUCATION AND AWARENESS

- run their own seminars and conferences

- establish trade hotline and referral services

- provide financial incentives to their industrial clients to explore exporting

- make personal calls on industrial clients

- team experienced exporters with novices for mentoring

INDUSTRY-SPECIFIC EXPORT DEVELOPMENT

- sponsor full-service training and technical assistance to a small "class" of the most promising industrial clients

- offer direct counseling

- compile a detailed, firm-specific database on existing and potential exporters in their service territories

- contract with overseas marketing consultants

- co-sponsor advertisements in trade journals on behalf of industrial clients branch and arrange financing for that order. In the United States, however, only a tiny fraction of the nation's 10,000 banks are capable of handling even currency transactions, much less export finance. Few banks even have staff skilled in export finance.

There are historical reasons for this situation. First, the American domestic market has been so big that, in the past, banks simply have not needed to take on the complexities, costs and risks of financing foreign transactions in order to make money. Second, many of the large commercial banks that once had international departments shut them down after the spectacular failure of large-scale development project investments in developing countries during the last decade and a half.

In the United States, few banks can handle foreign currency transactions— much less export finance. But this may be changing.

Today, those few U.S.-owned banks that do offer export financing typically are unwilling to finance deals under $500,000, largely because smaller deals have the same transaction costs as large ones but earn much smaller fees. Consequently, while some firms succeed in finding financing at the U.S. branches of foreign banks, the vast majority of small and medium-sized exporters must finance their deals internally or by requiring payment in advance. The U.S. Export-Import Bank, grossly underfunded when compared to similar institutions in other countries, is of little help in this predicament.

The commercial export-credit gap created by these conditions has had a severe dampening effect on U.S. exports. One survey found that banks met the export finance needs of no mid-sized firms and only 3 percent of small firms in the sample.[53] While internal financing may work for stable firms that have a negligible portion of their sales going to exports, cash flow constraints make this impractical for many serious exporters. Likewise, payment in advance works only for the lucky few firms not facing foreign competition, or for those whose foreign buyers are strongly committed to them because of their corporate relationships or other reasons.

But these conditions may be changing. Deregulation has increased competition in the banking industry. More banks are exploring export services—finance, research, marketing advice, referrals—as ways to attract customers who may use other, more profitable bank services.

Moreover, the National Export Strategy has made better export financing a priority. The U.S. Export-Import Bank and the Small Business Administration have retargeted and simplified their programs. Perhaps more important, they have given commercial banks new incentives and authority to write export loans guaranteed by the federal government. In addition, the federal government is restructuring its marketing efforts to train more banks in export finance and to enlist more partners at the state and local level who can help increase the awareness and utilization of federally assisted finance vehicles.

THE INDUSTRIAL MODERNIZATION CROWD DISCOVERS MARKETS

Two contemporary phenomena—the end of the Cold War and the growing pressures of international economic competition—have spawned two major domestic industrial-policy initiatives. First, defense facilities are being converted to new economic uses. Second, manufacturing is modernizing through new technology deployment, worker training and varying forms of interfirm cooperation. Significant new federal (and, in some cases, state) funds have been made available for such initiatives.

With their complementary focuses, technology and trade programs are—or should be— natural allies.

At the broadest level, these efforts seek to improve the competitiveness of the companies they assist. More specifically, they seek to improve the quality of products and the efficiency and productivity of manufacturers.

This often means, however, that these programs focus primarily on products and processes, not on *markets*. In the case of defense conversion efforts, this gap is perhaps explainable; defense industries, which developed and employed high-technology machinery and weapons, historically have had only a few customers.

But in a global economy, technology (including defense technology) and trade are highly interdependent. High-technology products are among the fastest-growing sectors in global trade. Moreover, technology products typically are niche products, requiring access to global markets to ensure an adequate customer base.

Traditional state trade programs tend to lack the ability to spot design or production problems that limit the exportability of a client firm's products. With their complementary focuses, technology and trade programs are—or should be—natural allies.

New Rules

For chronically underfunded and overstretched state trade offices, the new pressures placed on governance by changing conditions and players offer significant opportunities—for securing stable political, customer and financial support; for developing alliances and joint ventures that pool limited resources; for incorporating the imperative of internationalization into all economic development programs; and for helping more businesses more effectively.

Several states have used the opportunity to rethink the purpose, structure and operation of their trade promotion programs:

The new pressures placed on governance by changing conditions and players offer significant challenges and opportunities—and some states are taking them on.

- *New York* recently completely a comprehensive trade-strategy overhaul.

- *Wisconsin* created a public/private Export Strategy Commission to review and reform its approach to trade development.

- *Washington* established the post of state trade representative in the governor's office and sponsored the development of a statewide network of local trade-service providers to reach the most remote rural export-capable businesses.

- *North Carolina*—after a comprehensive review of public, private and nonprofit trade service and international education resources—

proposed the creation of a North Carolina International Commission. This body would not only develop a coherent state trade strategy and ensure efficient allocation of state resources for international programs, it would also coordinate advocacy at the state and federal levels, review international education programs, review cultural interaction programs and keep the state abreast of other states' initiatives.[54]

THE PRINCIPLES OF REINVENTION

Worthy as these efforts are, by and large they do not overcome the deep-seated problems inherent in the conventional system of top-down governmental services to businesses. Those problems—scale, fragmentation and accountability, among others—and the efforts of hard-pressed public sector officials to address them explain the success in 1992 of *Reinventing Government*, by David Osborne and Ted Gaebler.[55]

But worthy as their efforts are, most states have not overcome the deep-seated problems that are inherent in the conventional system of top-down governmental services to businesses.

Few states have taken the challenge of reinvention more seriously than Oregon. Under three consecutive governors and with the support of the legislature, the state has worked to overhaul every aspect of governance. It has established target performance benchmarks for programs of all kinds, made funding decisions based on that performance, and dramatically restructured its economic development department to focus on the specific objectives and needs of key industrial sectors and individual regions in the state. In the process, Oregon has jettisoned most of its former economic development programs.

Indeed, the state's Joint Legislative Committee on Trade and Economic Development recently boiled its entire agenda down to five simple but sweeping principles for organizing and carrying out market-driven approaches to economic development:

■■ Address the competitiveness of industries.

■■ Empower firms and groups of firms to solve their own problems.

- View the economy the way private firms do—by sector.

- Think strategically about which industries matter most to the state's economy.

- Put it all together in a system that uses industry associations, nonprofits and networks of firms—not just government programs—to connect public resources with business needs.[56]

If other states—and state trade programs—are to meet the challenges of the future with the resources of the present, if they are to overcome the problems of marginality, fragmentation, and accountability, they too must reenvision their purposes, their partners and their operating procedures. *(See "Oregon's Approach: Sales, Not Promotion" on page 41.)* The rules of the economic development game have changed, from programs to performance, from activities to outcomes. The balance of this report explores how a state might go about the process of reinventing its trade programs, integrating them into a coherent trade-development system, creating a capacity for managing its own foreign affairs, and strengthening its civic capacity for functioning as an international state. We begin with state trade programs.

> If states are to meet the challenges of the future with the resources of the present, they must reenvision their purposes, their partners and their procedures. Oregon has led the way.

Good salesmanship—and some state trade offices are very good sellers indeed—is not a trade development strategy. A trade promotion office, even a well-funded one, does not in and of itself make a state competitive internationally.

New Zealand, whose economy is on the scale of Arkansas or Kansas, develops an annual export strategy and progress report. Produced by the quasi-public New Zealand Trade Development Board (Tradenz), the plan incorporates sophisticated industry analysis and economic projections, evaluates developing trade challenges, profiles targeted industry sectors and markets, and presents a trade strategy. *(See "Tradenz: The New Zealand Trade Development Board" on next page.)*

The New Zealand trade strategy itself, which flows from the Tradenz analysis, is comprehensive. It considers program investments, financial infrastructure, new product development, education and skills training, benchmarking and the core competencies of *both* public and private sector trade institutions.

> **T**o be competitive, states need a comprehensive trade development *system,* not just a promotion program.

The trade strategy is, in short, one of the central organizing mechanisms of New Zealand's economic policy. Trade is not an afterthought—it is the *raison d'être* of economic development. Industrial modernization, workforce training, infrastructure development and capital access are important, in other words, *because* trade is important to economic advancement.

To be competitive, states need to think and act more like their competitors in other nations, not like their colleagues, the other states. They need to listen to their industrial customers and find ways to help them meet their own needs by mobilizing a wide array of public and private resources. They need, in short, a comprehensive trade development *system*, not just a promotion program.

Many components of such a system already are scattered across the economic development landscape. *(See Figure 8, page 58.)* They include not just the state economic development and agricultural trade offices, but also other agencies and elements of government that affect business competitiveness. They include many for-profit and nonprofit trade facilitators. And they include often overlooked representatives of foreign countries in each state, from consulates and embassies to resident aliens and exchange students.

TRADENZ:
THE NEW ZEALAND TRADE DEVELOPMENT BOARD[57]

In New Zealand, responsibility for trade development rests with Tradenz, a public-private board with the mission of helping New Zealand businesses increase foreign exchange earnings. To achieve this mission, Tradenz pursues two goals: *to substantially increase the value of New Zealand exports per capita* and *to diversify the range of exports.* Each goal can be measured—and both are, regularly.

The Board's mission statement specifically charges it to:

■ work with New Zealand exporters to identify and capitalize on market opportunities and improve their ability to compete profitably overseas

■ provide high-quality, cost-effective support and strategic advice to individual exporters

■ develop partnerships with industry groups (New Zealand has more than two dozen)

■ assist exporters by using its unique position between the public and private sectors to improve the conditions that can build international competitive advantage

■ build an export culture that will boost the confidence of exporters and enhance New Zealand's commitment to an export strategy

The conclusion of Tradenz's mission statement sets the stage for its design and accountability: *Our [organizational] culture is based on close interaction and identification with New Zealand exporters. We expect to be judged by the contribution that we make to the performance of New Zealand's foreign exchange earners.*

If states are to become competent competitors in a global economy, they will need to make sense of, and take full advantage of, these resources. In short, they should endeavor to internationalize all state business assistance programs and those other state programs that affect business competitiveness. To do so, they will need to start with a clear strategic vision.

The Launch: A Vision and Strategy Framework

The task of becoming an "international state" begins with the development of a statewide strategic planning process designed to produce a clear and coherent vision of how the state and its businesses will function—together—in a global economy.

This is a difficult first step. It is not simply a matter of bureaucratic integration, reorganization or program coordination, though these may be among the eventual results. It is a process that must be guided by and, ultimately, owned by industry itself, with state government facilitating, to the extent appropriate, and contributing what it is best suited to contribute: unvarnished analyses of the state's trade performance and competitive position, clear statements of public policy, technical assistance, and a willingness to work cooperatively with industry and the nonprofit sector where public policy and private sector goals meet.

Participants in such a process should include the administrators, private sector providers, and customers of trade services, as well as leaders in industrial modernization, education and training, agriculture, rural and urban development, finance, transportation and other strategic areas. Support for the strategic planning process should be sufficiently widespread that it will outlast the political fortunes of its immediate champions.

The outcome of the process is a policy framework for building and maintaining a world-class trade development and assistance system. This framework should include, at a minimum:

> The first step in becoming an "international state" is the development of a statewide strategic planning process designed to produce a clear and coherent vision of how the state and its businesses will function—together— in a global economy.

In 1990, the Florida state legislature established the Florida International Affairs Commission (FIAC) to function as a permanent, independent public-private body to support the international programs and policies of the state. Placed within the executive office of the governor, the commission is composed of 27 members in high-level public and private positions, 17 of whom are appointed by the governor.

MISSION

The FIAC is charged with the responsibility to:

- formulate state international policies and coordinate state programs and public and private activities relating to international affairs

- serve as a clearinghouse for program information

- establish a "think tank" for econometric and foreign political analysis

- develop program recommendations for export finance

- provide "one-stop" international information services

STRATEGIC PLAN

The legislation creating FIAC mandated the creation of a strategic plan for international trade and education. The plan was designed to establish for the state:

- quantifiable goals and objectives

- strategies to focus private and public resources

- criteria for performance evaluations

- policies to promote business and education ties with targeted foreign nations

- procedures to assure that education programs are adequate for understanding and participating in the global marketplace

- means to identify impediments in the state's tax structure and business climate

The cost for developing the strategic plan was about $85,000. Of this, $45,000 was spent on meetings of the FIAC board, various subordinate councils and the strategic planning committee (board and committee members donated their time). Another

$18,000 was spent on staff, $7,000 to hold public meetings around the state and $1,500 on printing and graphics. No special appropriation was needed; most of these costs were covered as part of FIAC's regular budget. FIAC's operating budget for 1994-95 was set at $635,000, funded through a percentage of a rental car surcharge.

■■ a clear, coherent *vision* statement

■■ a *focus* for all programs—trade, competitiveness and economic development—on firms and industries with strategic importance to the state's economy

■■ a frank *assessment* of state trade performance and foreign policy objectives

■■ specific, measurable *targets* for expanding foreign trade, strengthening trade infrastructure, improving statewide competency in languages and geographic literacy, and expanding foreign cultural contacts

■■ establishment of professional and institutionalized *networks* among stakeholders

■■ a commitment to invest in meaningful program *evaluation* and to base program and investment *adjustments* upon the results

■■ creation of a permanent deliberative body—with *public and private industry participation*—to monitor performance, regularly revisit the vision, and make adjustments as needed

Support for the strategic planning process should be sufficiently widespread that it will outlast the political fortunes of its immediate champions.

Two states—Florida and Hawaii—have made substantial progress in developing and sustaining statewide strategic plans for international development. Theirs are not simply export development programs, but comprehensive plans to internationalize the very fabric of commerce and society in their states. Each evolved under different circumstances and with different state champions. Hawaii's originated in the governor's office, whereas Florida's originated in the legislature. *(See "The Florida International Affairs Commission.")*

The Implementation: Eight Principles for Trade Assistance Delivery

In *Reinventing Government*, Osborne and Gaebler identify ten principles for "reinventing government"—that is, for overcoming the inherent limitations of direct service delivery by government.[58] These principles offer a useful framework for rethinking the structure and operation of state trade programs and for overcoming the growing problems of marginality, fragmentation and accountability in the delivery of trade assistance services.

The ten Osborne/Gaebler principles and how they apply to trade assistance are detailed in Figure 9. In the text below, they are synthesized into eight principles for state trade-service delivery, with some examples of how the principles might be put into practice.

More than simply export development programs, what is needed are comprehensive strategic plans to internationalize the very fabric of states' commerce and society.

1. A MISSION-DRIVEN TRADE SERVICES SYSTEM

Most state trade-program mission statements, such as they are, simply exhort the program to "increase exports and recruit foreign investment." But, with respect to the former, when asked whether their strategy is to increase the *number* of exporters in the state or the *value* of the state's exports, many state trade officers reply, "Both."

It is an understandable but technically impossible response. The political system within which state trade offices operate typically prohibits the kind of triage that would permit state trade directors to decide who will be served, who will not, and why. And the executive and legislative mandates under which they operate often are too vague (or too contradictory) to give them the

76

FIGURE 9. **REINVENTION PRINCIPLES AND TRADE ASSISTANCE**[59]

REINVENTION PRINCIPLE	HOW IT APPLIES TO TRADE ASSISTANCE
Mission-Driven	Clearly articulate trade development objectives and operating principles
Anticipatory	Improve long-term strategy development to anticipate shifts in global markets
Market-Oriented	Think in terms of supply and demand, rather than "programs"
Customer-Led	Ignore previous mandates or existing programs and base services on current client-articulated needs
Catalytic	Mobilize existing service providers, rather than provide all services directly
Competitive	Encourage competition among public and private trade-service organizations to provide demanded services, based on quality and expertise, not past contracting history or mandates
Empowering	Help industrial sector organizations take ownership of and responsibility for changing business (and government) behavior about trade
Decentralized	Ensure that trade assistance services are designed and delivered as close as is practical to the targeted businesses
Enterprising	Establish fees for services, commissions, cash matching contributions, soft loans and so forth
Results-Oriented	Measure and base program funding on actual outcomes, not levels of activity; reward innovation

77

statutory foundation or political cover they need for making such tough decisions.

The result is trade offices with limited resources that must be spread too thin to make much of a difference on either front—number of exporters *or* value of exports. The plain fact is that the tactics associated with these two potential strategic goals differ sharply, and no state has the fiscal resources to pursue both either simultaneously or effectively.

In the absence of a clear, delineated mission, a state trade program can't be certain where it is going or whether it is making progress. It can occupy itself with activities and events, but will have difficulty demonstrating that those activities are having any impact. Although many state trade offices boast staff with technical expertise; that is not enough either. The strategic issue is how they will apply that expertise, where, with whom, and to what purpose.

To answer these questions, state trade offices must have clear mission statements that lay out their operating principles and articulate their objectives in measurable terms. Setting performance benchmarks is critical to defining expected progress; for example, "Half of all mid-sized manufacturers will export within five years." Without detailing an agency's mission in this way, staff can develop no criteria for apportioning resources strategically. Without such criteria, they are left at the mercy of chance and, more troubling, persistent political manipulation.

> **In the absence of a clear, delineated mission, a state trade program can't be certain where it is going or whether it is making progress.**

Finally, in a world of multiple public and private sector export-service providers, the absence of such clarity means that there is no mechanism for determining the shape of alliances or the distribution of services among members. Fragmentation and marginal impact are perpetuated, not resolved.

2. AN ANTICIPATORY TRADE-SERVICES SYSTEM

For a trade development strategy to be a functioning, adaptive trade-services delivery system, it must be able, among other things, to anticipate shifts in global markets, industry trends, emerging competition, even changes in public policy. It must be able to see the future as it advances over the horizon. To do so, a state trade office needs access to professional research capacity. Without intelligence-gathering capabilities, the strategy—and the state's businesses—are likely to be blind-sided or simply overtaken by events.

Yet few states have such capacity. It's not surprising. Neither legislatures nor most governors place much priority on research or planning (until a crisis arises), and state trade offices themselves are so driven by the annual calendar of trade-related events that looking ahead seems a luxury for which they have little time.

Operating without quality research and analysis, however, risks more than simply failing to anticipate emerging opportunities or problems. It also risks failing to learn from the past. High staff turnover and uneven recordkeeping leave many trade offices with neither an institutional memory nor, more importantly, baselines against which to measure their own progress. In the absence of such baselines and the measurements they afford, it is difficult to argue persuasively for support at budget time.

Several states have flirted with providing analytic support for their trade services programs. Virginia, for example, has intermittently invested in trade staff who have analytic skills. Minnesota has a research office in the Department of Trade and Economic Development that produces factbooks for the trade division. Maryland does a better job than many other states at keeping track of trade performance, but a university-initiated "report card" on trade lapsed when its champion left the state.

Yet even these efforts have largely failed at the broader task of keeping the trade assistance operation regularly apprised of opportunities and updated on performance. Without such intelligence, and the ability to modify services accordingly, a trade development strategy threatens to begin ossifying from the moment it is first presented. It is, if not dead on arrival, then dying from the moment of birth.

> **W**ithout intelligence-gathering capabilities, the state's trade development strategy— and the state's businesses— are likely to be blind-sided or simply overtaken by events.

3. A MARKET-ORIENTED, CUSTOMER-LED TRADE SERVICES SYSTEM

As Corporation for Enterprise Development analysis has observed, economic development programs and, for that matter, state trade-promotion programs, often are created "because of a *presumption* that a particular type of business service is important."[60] Sometimes the presumption arises from a felt public policy need, like the need to create more better-paying jobs. Sometimes it arises from a widely asserted but inadequately analyzed problem, like a lack of awareness among smaller firms about the "need to be globally competitive." These presumed needs are translated into legislative mandates and programmatic responses, often with considerable (if short-lived) fanfare.

Rigorous customer targeting is still relatively rare. Broad agency mandates and persistent political pressure to help whoever walks in the door make it difficult for trade programs to target customers.

The results, however, are almost always disappointing, because such initiatives seldom arise from an *analysis*— of gaps in public or private services, of the ability of government agencies to mount an effective response, or even of the targeted firms or industries themselves. In most states, there is no market mechanism for determining the demand for trade assistance services or, for that matter, for analyzing the supply of such services in the state. The few existing customer surveys used by state trade offices tend to query only past users of government services, not potential customers in a targeted customer pool.

There is some evidence, however, that this is changing. Idaho surveys 8,000-10,000 firms by industry category every year to determine whether they currently export or are interested in exporting.[61] For some years, Oregon's trade division has conducted periodic "community sweeps" to identify firms with potential. To help staff aim services at the right customers, firms have then been sorted into four categories:

▪▪ firms ready for an international project

▪▪ firms that will be ready within the current biennium

▪▪ firms that will not be ready within the current biennium

·▪ firms that are unlikely ever to enter active exporting, despite their potential[62]

Yet rigorous customer targeting is still relatively rare. Broad agency mandates and persistent political pressure to help whoever walks in the door make it difficult for trade programs to target customers. Former Washington state trade director Jeanne Cobb DeMund explains the problem: "Using studies on market and product trends, we try to focus on firms in key industries best equipped to penetrate target markets. We know whom we want to serve; the problem is we aren't very good at saying no to others."[63] Colorado's trade director echoes her conclusion: "We're still pretty sloppy about screening out un-serious firms," says Morgan Smith.[64]

And yet sharply limited resources and an increased demand to demonstrate performance are leading more and more state leaders to set aside old mandates and programmatic presumptions in favor of customer-led trade services. At a minimum, a state trade office should be able to answer, in specific terms, three basic questions about its customer base:

> **A**t a minimum, a state trade office should be able to answer three basic questions: Who are its customers, what are their needs, and who can best fill those needs?

·▪ *Who is the customer?* Is it small, medium or large firms? Existing exporters with growth potential, infrequent exporters or non-exporters? Targeted sectors or any-and-all-comers? Who produces high-value, exportable products and services and where are they?

·▪ *What are the customer's needs?* Is it generic education and information about export opportunities, or technical assistance tailored to a specific product, market or transaction? Are the barriers the customer faces trade-related or more fundamental—involving production modernization or workforce training, for example? How do targeted firms learn and from whom? And what have firms that have exported successfully without public assistance (the vast majority) learned that might increase the value of assistance given to new or would-be exporters?

·▪ *Which organizations are best equipped to meet these customer needs?* Should the state trade office attempt to be both a generalist and a specialist? What other public, nonprofit and private sector organizations provide or claim to provide export assistance, and what are their core competencies?

4. A CATALYTIC AND COMPETITIVE PUBLIC-PRIVATE TRADE SERVICES SYSTEM

What matters most in the internationalization of a state economy are the needs of firms and the development of a system for meeting them. In any state, just as company needs for export services cover a broad spectrum from the most generic to the most specific, so too is there a spectrum of export service providers—public, private and nonprofit. In most states, even though these providers typically chase the same customers and offer them an array of virtually identical services broader than either their resources or expertise, they remain locked in direct, costly and continuous competition with each other. Ad hoc coordinating bodies, organized a few years ago amid the sudden and, in retrospect, shallow vogue for "public-private partnerships," have rarely done much to remedy this situation.

Even the best-financed state trade-assistance program can meet only some of the needs of only a fraction of export-capable firms

Even the best-financed state trade-assistance program can meet only some of the needs of only a fraction of export-capable firms—thus placing the public policy objective of dramatically expanded exports beyond the reach of a state program acting alone. Hence, it is in the state's interest to leverage its resources by helping the range of private for-profit and nonprofit entities—industry associations, chambers of commerce, world trade centers, port authorities, financial institutions and private trade consultants, among others—to become skilled and active in delivering trade assistance services to firms.

And since these private and nonprofit sector organizations face essentially the same bleak realities of limited resources and skills as the state, it is in their interest to cooperate in such an endeavor. States thus have an extraordinary opportunity to catalyze an entirely new approach to trade development—one that identifies the core competencies of the array of service providers, matches them with the needs of targeted customers, and seeks to fill the gaps in the spectrum or get someone else to fill them.

In short, while state trade offices may continue to provide direct services, though under much more clearly defined performance criteria, the long-term objective must be to facilitate the development of a statewide system of service providers.

One way to approach this task is to organize providers and services to suit different types of customers. There are, in one sense, two categories of customers:

T he long-term objective of every state trade-assistance program should be to facilitate the development of a statewide system of service providers.

■■ *Export-ready.* One category includes those firms that are ready to pay market rates for professional technical assistance—and who need only to be connected to the right providers.

■■ *Export-unready.* The second category consists of firms that are inexperienced in exporting, those that export only intermittently, and those nonexporting companies still so uncertain or uncommitted that they require more nurturing and guidance before they can export independently. The latter generally are unwilling to commit significant resources to what they perceive as a risky and long-term project. If the state's objective is to increase the number of exporters, these firms will always require an initial public subsidy. They may be willing to pay modest fees, or even commissions on future sales to offset that subsidy, but they are unready to purchase services on the open market, presuming such services are available.

Given this division of firms, a state interested in operating as a catalyst could help organize existing nonstate technical service providers, based upon their strongest expertise, and direct qualified firms to them. At the same time, the state could take on the task of providing opportunities for unready firms to acquire the level of experience or interest necessary to pursue exporting.

Perhaps the simplest mechanism for engaging existing private sector organizations in this enterprise—and for getting them to focus on their strengths—would be to inject an element of competition. A state commerce department could issue a request for proposals for organizations capable of providing export services to export-ready firms. In lieu of direct state-program delivery, it could then contract with the organizations that demonstrate the greatest skill to provide services.

Over time, more organizations will seek participation in this joint venture with the state, not only to access the export-ready customer base, but because down the line, the state will have them in mind when it refers newly qualified firms, made export-ready by the state's own trade services, to outside providers. Such a system places the state in a catalyzing role. It strengthens the skills of private and quasi-private sector organizations, and in the process improves the quality of services available to customers. It combines the limited resources of each trade services provider to form a coherent critical mass that replaces fragmentation and confusion.

> **A** state interested in acting as a catalyst can help organize existing non-state technical service providers, based on their expertise, and direct qualified firms to them.

5. A SYSTEM THAT HELPS INDUSTRY HELP ITSELF

At their core, state economic development programs are all about trying to provide citizens with opportunities for a better life. State trade-assistance programs have the same solid intentions. The state seeks to make firms aware of the need to be globally competitive—in part through trade—because it wants companies to grow robustly and create good, well-paying jobs for citizens. So it creates programs to help firms meet those goals and encourages firms to utilize the programs.

That firms typically do not avail themselves of these services demonstrates that businesses simply do not think of government as a solution when they have a problem. Rightly or wrongly, they perceive government as inaccessible, unresponsive, inflexible, cumbersome and, most importantly, ignorant of their particular industry and needs.

Similarly, business leaders are far less likely to adopt a new idea when it is promoted by government than when it is promoted by someone in their own industry. This is not so much because they are suspicious of government intentions as that they simply do not perceive government as a credible source. Research on export-related problems shows firms are far more likely to turn to contacts in their own industry, or elsewhere in the private sector, than to the state.[65]

Indeed, despite promotional campaigns, firms are generally unaware of government export-assistance programs. This may be because businesses "belong," in a sense, to industry sectors; they have no similar sense of affinity with government programs. They believe that colleagues and competitors in their industry sector can grasp their problems, speak their language, and understand the specifics of their businesses. Correctly or not, they perceive that private sector initiatives will be more creative, responsive and relevant to their needs than government programs: Whereas government agencies may offer *services, their* own industries offer *solutions.* The fact that many industries are not organized to provide such solutions does not seem to alter this perception; it is deeply ingrained.

> **O**ne obstacle that states face is that, despite promotional campaigns, firms are generally unaware of or uninterested in government export-assistance programs.

Given these realities, state export-development objectives are more likely to be achieved if export assistance services are delivered to, and through, groups of firms within industry sectors. This approach is crucial for several reasons. First, by working with and through industry groups, firms themselves gain a sense of ownership in the enterprise, and ownership breeds commitment and credibility. Second, by having this sense of ownership, industry becomes not simply a "client" but an advocate for trade development services. That advocacy is crucial for achieving a measure of insulation from electoral politics and, more importantly, consistent and stable financial support for trade services. Third, by shifting the locus of state export-assistance investments from individual firms to groups of firms, states can begin to overcome the lack-of-scale problem—that is, their inability to provide direct, detailed assistance to more than a few companies each year.

This shift to industry empowerment and ownership is already under way in a few locales:

- The state of *Oregon* has completely reorganized its economic development programs around industry sectors identified as having strategic importance to the state. It provides modest financial incentives for firms in those industries to organize to help themselves. The companies define their own development agenda, identify their own needs (which typically include export market development) and draw up plans for meeting those needs with their own and the state's resources.

- In Canada, the *British Columbia* Trade Development Corporation has gone even further, structuring much of its trade assistance program around the needs of industry-formed export networks—or groups of firms. Some 500 firms are now organized in networks within 16 industry subsectors.[66] *(See "British Columbia: An Export Network System.")*

BRITISH COLUMBIA: AN EXPORT NETWORK SYSTEM[67]

The British Columbia Trade Development Corporation (B.C. Trade), a "Crown" corporation owned by the provincial government, has been mandated to promote the export of goods and services from British Columbia. To do so, it has had to deal with the international marketing challenges faced by the many small and medium-sized enterprises (SMEs) in the province, a daunting challenge in itself.

Accepting that challenge, B.C. Trade has devised one of the most innovative trade development strategies in North America. The basis of its strategy is the "flexible business network," a self-selected group of SME firms that mobilize their collective resources in a flexible structure organized around their industrial sector or around a common international market or project.

Today, British Columbia is home to 16 flexible networks involving nearly 500 SMEs. Working together in their networks, these firms have assembled the capabilities and clout to compete in international markets, markets dominated by large multinationals and, increasingly, the business networks of other nations.

HOW NETWORKS WORK FOR FIRMS

The flexible network provides more than a means to enhance

competitiveness and stimulate economic activity; it provides a way to compensate for the inherent weaknesses of small firms. Participating in a flexible network enables SMEs to:

- *Increase management depth*. As the pool of talent within a network expands, so do ideas about how to better administer company activities.

- *Locate and use market information*. Collective resources increase the timeliness and accuracy of market intelligence.

- *Keep pace with change*. Members of flexible networks become more familiar with the competition, both domestic and international.

- *Access funds for R&D and market development*. Pooling funds affords network members financial clout they would otherwise lack.

- *Gain experience in export markets*. For example, one member's knowledge of the Latin American market becomes the network's knowledge.

- *Access capital*. Networks provide a "critical financial mass" for going after capital that in-dividual companies could never hope to secure.

In short, focused cooperation affords network members competitive advantages of scale, scope and speed.

HOW B.C. TRADE WORKS FOR NETWORKS

The 16 networks that have coalesced in British Columbia over the past five years have been effectively "brokered"—that is, organized with facilitated discussions—by B.C. Trade. Each has followed the same three-phase development model. Initially, after identifying a specific opportunity for collaboration, a feasibility study is conducted. If the project is determined feasible, a business plan is developed that specifies the network's purposes and objectives. The final phase is implementation.

British Columbia's flexible networks have been developed from B.C. Trade's client base. Although most continue to lean on B.C. Trade funds to help pay for brokering services, one of the 16 networks already has become entirely self-sufficient.

■■ *Denmark*, with an economy smaller than many states, is in its third round of fostering export networks nationwide. Denmark provides matching grants and loans totaling some $13 million to groups of firms that organize themselves to achieve export objectives.[68]

6. A DECENTRALIZED TRADE-SERVICES SYSTEM

To be effective, export services must be more than simply available somewhere in the state; it helps if service providers and decisionmaking are decentralized, that is, geographically close to the targeted firms. This helps not only by providing time-sensitive and overworked firm owners easier access; it also offers more opportunity for business leaders to help design services, and ensures that service providers are "grounded" in the realities that firms face.

To be effective, service providers and decisionmaking should be decentralized— and this is especially crucial for rural firms.

The need for decentralization is especially crucial for rural firms. The plain fact is that most of the businesses in any state are located in metropolitan areas—and the available export services, in general, thus tend to be concentrated in state capitals or major cities. Yet rural economies are, by and large, no longer dominated by commodity production; many are now manufacturing economies. And rural manufacturers, because they tend to be poorly equipped to compete globally, are prime targets for a state's export-awareness and prep services.[69]

Few states have the resources to support decentralized service delivery on their own. A phone survey of trade programs in states west of the Mississippi revealed that only two, Minnesota and Washington, had an explicit strategy for reaching rural businesses. Oregon, as noted earlier, conducts periodic "community sweeps" around the state to find export-capable firms, and Idaho trade staff participate in regional economic-development agency teams that visit remote parts of the state from time to time. But most states, when asked how they are addressing the international market development opportunities of rural businesses, comment either that they serve the entire state (therefore, including rural

88

areas) or that there are not enough rural businesses with exportable products to warrant a special outreach program. They offer no data, however, to support these assertions.[70]

While some states are addressing this problem with initiatives to modernize manufacturing, few have incorporated international-market development as a central component of these initiatives. If rural economies are to escape a downward spiral, rural manufacturers must look beyond traditional markets.

Road shows and occasional forays into the hinterlands can do much to raise awareness both of the challenges of global competition and the opportunity for foreign sales markets, but unless assistance is accessible and, more important, sustained over time, rural firms are unlikely to become traders. An integrated state system of central trade offices and regional providers of technical assistance could help fill those gaps.

At some point in the not-too-distant future, telecommunication options will facilitate decentralizing more export assistance services.

It may well be that at some point in the not-too-distant future, telecommunication options will enable the decentralization of more export assistance services. Georgia, for example, is developing a video-conferencing network that can link a rural site with up to eight other sites, including the central state trade office and overseas offices. The state will use this system for service coordination and technical assistance, as well as for online discussions between the potential buyers visiting Georgia's booth at an overseas trade show and Georgia businesses back home. At present, however, the most effective mechanism may be to combine the forces of substate regional economic-development organizations, local chambers of commerce, and technical or community colleges to function as service delivery "nodes"—local points of access to professional services for rural firms.

Wisconsin is currently considering such an approach, and the state of Washington has recently created a Local Trade Assistance Network— ten local organizations, chosen competitively, that will provide export assistance services in rural areas. *(See "Washington State: A Local Trade Assistance Network.")*

89

In 1994, the state of Washington launched an International Trade Initiative that elevated trade development and export service delivery to a statewide economic development priority. As one part of the initiative, the state created a Local Trade Assistance Network designed to ensure that hands-on export trade-assistance services were available to small and medium-sized businesses in rural areas of the state.

The state awarded modest matching grants, totaling nearly $500,000—ranging from $23,000 to $85,000 each—to ten substate regional organizations, now referred to as the Local Trade Assistance Network. The competitive grants went to the groups who offered the best proposals for bringing together existing export services, both public and private, and delivering them locally to rural firms.

After identifying businesses in their regions that have export potential, the Local Trade Assistance Network providers will:

- assess each firm's export readiness

- produce tailored market research and customized country-specific market plans

- find overseas distributors and buyers

- qualify trade leads

- help firms meet custom standards and shipping documentation requirements

- provide referrals for translation, freight forwarding, and finance services

The initiative, currently planned to last three years, is unique in the nation for two reasons. First, it represents an unusually well-planned, decentralized, rural service-delivery effort. Second, it is jointly designed, funded and managed by the state's Departments of Agriculture and Community, Trade and Economic Development—agencies that compete with each other in most other states.

7. AN ENTERPRISING TRADE-SERVICES SYSTEM

An enterprising export-services system aims to strengthen market mechanisms wherever possible and to function in businesslike ways.

It resorts to direct state action only to fill service gaps—and even then only until the market can be restructured to fill those gaps on its own.

From the start, subsidies have been part and parcel of state export-promotion programs: free counseling, cheap seminars, subsidized trade-fair participation and trade missions, below-market fees for export transaction assistance, assistance in obtaining export finance and the like. In this climate, neither staff nor clients are subject to the disciplines of the marketplace.

State trade programs should resort to direct state action only to fill service gaps— and even then only until the market can be restructured to fill those gaps on its own.

Trade service redesigners can start to address this situation by considering two questions:

■■ *First, do state personnel possess enough expertise, and command enough trust, to advise businesses beyond the level of basic data and referrals?*

A reinvented state trade program might aim to contract with private and nonprofit organizations better suited to delivering tailored services. The role of government, in this case, would be to establish performance criteria, provide training if necessary, and offer direct services only when nongovernmental providers do not exist or yet recognize the market opportunity.

■■ *Second, what is the state's rationale for providing valuable services to businesses for free, or at substantially subsidized rates?*

In one respect at least, public subsidies are inevitable. As long as it is an objective of public policy to recruit and train new firms for exporting—firms that otherwise would not participate—tax dollars will be required. Trade service providers commonly report that small nonexporting firms will not pay market rates for export assistance until it has been demonstrated to them that exporting pays. Firms may pay a nominal fee to attend an export opportunity seminar, but that's it. Even enthusiastic encouragement by government export promoters will not alter this reality.

At the other extreme, frequent exporters regularly purchase market development services from private sector providers. For them, it is a normal cost of doing business, and subsidy is totally unnecessary.

91

In between these two extremes, however, there is much room for reforming state trade programs so that they operate in a more business-like, more enterprising manner. Many states are moving, albeit tentatively, towards an operating policy that posits: If export assistance is worth receiving, it is worth paying for to some degree. Even ignoring the pressures of budget limitations, these innovators see little justification for providing taxpayer-supported business assistance services free or at substantially discounted prices.

Moreover, the establishment of fees and other cost-recovery mechanisms screens out the nonserious "dabblers." Paying extracts a level of commitment from firms that grants do not, and creates a market test for the service provided. If companies value the service, they will pay for it; if they do not, government should question why it is offering the service in the first place. "It's scary," former Oregon trade division director Glenn Ford notes, "because you never know whether you have a service customers really want until you ask them to pay for it."[71]

> **Many states are moving, albeit tentatively, towards a policy that posits: If export assistance is worth receiving, it is worth paying for to some degree.**

More for budgetary than policy reasons, most state trade offices now charge fees for many of the services they provide. But these fees often are deeply discounted and constitute a limited vision of enterprise. For export-willing firms that are committed to formulating and executing an export-market development strategy, other options should be available. At a minimum, any financial assistance offered by the state to a firm should require a hefty match—in cash, not in "in-kind" services.

Beyond this, if upfront fees constitute too great a financial burden for a small, inexperienced would-be exporter, "soft loans" or commission contracts are an intriguing option. The Oregon Joint Legislative Committee on Trade and Economic Development has considered soft loans for export market development:

> *A "soft loan" program for market development would work as follows. The government would lend private businesses some portion of the cost of market exploration and development, reimbursing a*

portion of out-of-pocket costs incurred for travel, lodging, trade show attendance, interpreters, market studies and so on. If the firm actually exports its goods or services, the loan has to be repaid, typically at market rates. If the firm does not succeed in selling exports over some stated period of time, the loan is forgiven. The program lowers the cost and risk associated with seeking new markets. The program would require the preparation of an export development plan and some up-front fee to discourage nonserious inquiries or possible abuse.[72]

As a variant of soft loans, state trade offices can execute sales commission or royalty agreements by which the state's investment in export assistance is repaid—at market interest rates—once participating companies make sales abroad. Some state trade offices have claimed their customers would never divulge their export sales figures so commissions could be charged against them, but this problem is readily solved by executing a simple formal contract.

> **If upfront fees constitute too great a financial burden for a small, inexperienced would-be exporter, "soft loans" or commission contracts are an option to consider.**

Oregon, in fact, has been operating a version of contract-based trade assistance for years. The state of Washington's Pacific Northwest Export Assistance Project, a quasi-public export technical-assistance program, also functioned on a contract basis until its contract expired at the end of 1995. Ohio has launched the Ohio Export Assistance Network, which relies heavily on fees, commissions and corporate contributions to supplement a state investment in start-up costs. *(See "Ohio Export Assistance Network.")* Other states, like Wisconsin, are considering similar initiatives.

What happens to fees once they've been collected is another problem. Fees simply returned to a state's general fund create no incentive within the agency to innovate. Moreover, as Mike Doyle of Iowa's international division notes, "When you start earning fees, someone in the legislature is always going to want to cut your budget." Iowa tries to solve this problem by depositing its net fee income in the Iowa Development Foundation, a nonprofit organization created some years ago to take on trade-related tasks that government agencies often can't perform for legal or political reasons—like entertaining foreign dignitaries.[73]

93

The Ohio Export Assistance Network (OEAN) is a public-private partnership structured as a not-for-profit corporation. OEAN behaves like a hard-boiled private company, but exists for public purposes. Launched as an experimental business venture, OEAN's mission is to fill a specific gap in the state's trade system. As such, the OEAN is designed to complement the existing service structure—it does not seek to replace programs.

OEAN targets small and medium-sized "export-ready" companies. The assessment of "export readiness" is based more on character, however, than on statistics.

OEAN has three basic levels of services:

■ The first level is *pre-export development* for companies that have exportable products but lack adequate management, capital structure, marketing approach or engineering. OEAN does not accept these companies as clients until they are "stabilized," but it helps them navigate through the business assistance system.

■ The second level is *direct assistance*. Each client receives a customized program of training, research and transactional assistance that reflects its stage of export maturity. OEAN sticks with the client until the firm is self-sufficient in selling to international markets.

■ The third level of service is forming *industry strategic alliances*. OEAN will organize an industry group that can produce the volume and breadth of product offerings to fill a market niche OEAN has identified.

With a state grant of about $400,000 to cover its two-year start-up period, OEAN opened its doors in November 1994. In addition to its service mix, four features set OEAN apart from most other trade development programs:

■ *Board Structure.* OEAN has the look and feel of a private sector company. The seven-member board has no representation from nonprofit organizations. Only one member acts as liaison to the public sector—the director of the Ohio Department of Economic Development. The other six members are from a variety of the state's top industries.

- *Funding and Performance Expectations.* OEAN recognizes that export counseling for smaller, new-to-export companies will never be self-financing. Continuation of state support will depend on the demonstration of a few successes, but OEAN has tried to keep expectations in line with reality.

  With the hope of eliminating its reliance on state funding, OEAN is actively soliciting contributions from corporations, especially geographic stakeholding companies, like banks and utilities, that stand to gain from the network's export successes. Client service fees, both flat fees and commissions, will make up another core source of funding.

- *Staff and Workload.* Each OEAN trade advisor is limited to a caseload of no more than five clients at any given time. Given that OEAN expects clients to stay with it for anywhere from six months to three years, this means staff have the chance to develop very close relationships with their clients. The idea is to aim for high service quality and big results.

- *Client Relations.* To foster client trust, OEAN pitches its trade advisors as loaned executives. Indeed, the staff do come straight from industry, with no public program experience. OEAN also takes care to avoid using the "Hello, I'm from the government..." behaviors that business people often scorn, such as over-structured interviews. Trade staff also wear beepers and carry laptop computers so they can help their clients at a moment's notice.

Some private export consultants have complained that state-subsidized trade services constitute unfair competition, but here too an enterprising solution is available—one, in fact, that can strengthen the entire system of service providers. To make a profit, private-sector trade consultants need qualified customers, that is, customers who are committed to pursuing a market opportunity and sufficiently knowledgeable to do so effectively. State trade offices could define their task as helping nonexporters and inexperienced exporters prepare for and negotiate their *first* overseas sale, after which the state refers them to qualified private sector export-service providers. Once again, it is in the interest of the state to help support the entry of firms into exporting, but not to subsidize them once they have "learned the ropes."

8. A RESULTS-ORIENTED TRADE SERVICES SYSTEM

Few state trade offices have a very clear idea about how well they are doing. As detailed earlier, in part this is because many trade agencies do not state their goals in measurable terms. Many goals are vague, and merely assert that firms will become exporters, or that current exporters will increase sales and create new jobs. By contrast, Idaho specifies in its international business plan the expected growth, by a certain date, in the dollar value of export sales and in the number of exporting companies.

The inability to provide well-documented outcome data can cripple and even kill state trade programs.

Officials have gotten by with vague goals because state trade offices can usually point with pride to a few exemplary firms that have added sales or created new jobs thanks to the state's help in identifying new markets overseas. More often than not, however, the information available has more to do with *activity*—the numbers of trade missions taken, firms at trade fairs, counseling sessions given, seminars offered and the like—than with *outcomes* like job creation, sales or new joint ventures, even though it is outcomes that firms and citizens really care about.

Moreover, when sales or job creation results are presented, the numbers are frequently unreliable. This is a problem inherent in economic development, not just trade development. "On average," says Blaine Liner, who evaluates state programs for the Urban Institute's State Policy Center, "the touted outcomes are about 30 to 50 percent inflated."[74]

The problem of measuring progress is complicated, of course, by the fact that trade development by its very nature is a messy, drawn-out and uncertain business that often involves multiple players. In many cases, it is nearly impossible to connect effects to causes. Morgan Smith, Colorado's trade director, echoes many of his colleagues: "We know there has been significant trade growth, but it's hard for us to claim credit for it directly."[75]

It is also the case that trade directors' superiors in the legislative and executive branches of state government rarely demonstrate either an interest in evaluation or a willingness to fund the work necessary to track actual results. "Our legislators don't care and don't understand the information on trade results when it's presented to them," one state trade director commented at a recent national meeting. Says Peter Cunningham, Nevada's trade director, "In a small state with a small trade budget, evaluation falls to the bottom every time."[76]

The problem of measuring progress is complicated by the fact that trade development by its very nature is a messy, drawn-out and uncertain business that often involves multiple players.

Perhaps ironically, the inability to provide well-documented *outcome* data can cripple and even kill state trade programs. A legislative audit of Maryland's trade program nearly led to its elimination in 1992 when the legislature found its claimed results were exaggerated. More often, however, the impact is less dramatic. As Washington agricultural export promotion specialist Eric Hurlbert explains: "We never really audited our trade development numbers; maybe that's why we're down to one person from a staff of 16 a few years ago."[77] Here again, the problem is typically the quality of the information, not the sincerity of intent.

In the absence of an outcome measurement system, trade offices have to rely on the information given to them by the firms they help. Often, the firms hope for greater trade-induced growth than is actually realized. Iowa's Mike Doyle explains: "Companies overstate their projected sales to please us; it's taken us a while to get them to understand that isn't helpful."[78]

But this result is not inevitable. States are beginning to demand outcome information from their clients, often as a precondition for receiving assistance:

■■ *Kansas*, for example, requires firms that receive funding assistance for trade show participation to report on their follow-up activities immediately after the show and at six- and twelve-month intervals.

■■ *Iowa* requires written results immediately following the event and then conducts follow-up calls after six months and again after one year.

■■ *Texas* tracks the progress of customers it serves at six-week, three-month, six-month and twelve-month intervals. Firms, which are guaranteed confidentiality not just for themselves but for their overseas customers, provide written reports on new sales in specific market regions. As a consequence, the state trade office is able to produce for the legislature an "efficiency rating" that illustrates the sales impact of export assistance per dollar spent.

■■ Follow-up calls work, *Iowa's* Doyle says: "Where we do follow-up calls, total sales are much higher than where we do not. The problem is getting the legislature to fund unglamorous work; they prefer to fund events."[79]

As the Corporation for Enterprise Development has noted, "Program evaluation is program development."[80] Unless a development assistance organization knows what is working and what is not, it cannot know whether it is serving its clients well. Put another way, it may know how fast it is walking, but not whether it is getting anywhere.

> **U**nless a trade assistance organization knows what is working and what is not, it cannot know whether it is serving its clients well.

If the crisis in state budgets during the late 1980s and early 1990s has achieved anything, it is that more and more states are trying to figure out whether they *are* getting anywhere. One example: Oregon's Benchmarks program, a system of detailed outcome targets for virtually every segment of the state's development program, is certainly the most comprehensive performance-monitoring program in the nation. (In Oregon's vocabulary, *benchmarks* serve as long-term goals, *performance measures* track progress towards them. *See Figure 10 for a list of suggested trade and competitiveness performance measures.*)

Less sweeping efforts to develop more precise business plans for development agencies, with more concrete outcome goals, are emerging nationwide. Several state trade offices have begun developing "return on investment" data for their governors or legislatures:

Here are examples of measures that agencies could track over time to assess the performance and outcomes of their trade assistance and international development efforts.

TRADE PERFORMANCE

- the dollar value of manufacturing exports divided by state population, total state production workforce, total shipments or gross state product

- growth rates for total state manufactured exports, over three- or five-year intervals

- state shares of contracts with multilateral development banks

- export growth rates by key industrial sector (at three- or four-digit SIC code level)

- global market shares by key industrial sector

- percent of firms exporting, by size of firm

- percent of manufacturing employment related to manufactured exports

- percent of total civilian employment related to manufactured exports

- percent of workforce in export-intensive industries

FOREIGN DIRECT INVESTMENT (FDI) AND OUTREACH INVESTMENT

- total FDI in the state, perhaps relative to other states

- FDI in new plants and plant expansions

- number of joint ventures involving state firms (or those in key markets)

CIVIC/EDUCATIONAL CAPACITY

- percent of students in foreign-language classes

- numbers of foreign students in state institutions of higher education

- percent of state students studying abroad

- state share of temporary foreign visitors coming to the United States for business

- percent of faculty working overseas

- number of Sister City pairs

(continued on next page)

99

- number of diplomatic linkages (consulates, honorary consuls, AID-funded links)

- percentage of a state's citizens who have passports

- total legal immigrant population shares

- frequency of major articles about the state in the *Economist* and *Financial Times*

PHYSICAL INFRASTRUCTURE

- volume of air and port cargo shipments

- volume of international passenger traffic originating in the state

- number of international flight slots at airports in the state

- changes in shipping calls (in port states)

TECHNOLOGY

- percent of manufacturers with ISO 9000 registration

- number of university research linkages abroad

- number of patents held abroad by in-state residents

- number of foreign delegations of scientists and technology-related officials

- Internet access and usage in the state

BUSINESS INFRASTRUCTURE

- business opinions of the trade support system, as measured in regular polls

- accessibility of advanced-trade legal and consulting services

- volume of export deals financed through in-state commercial banks

- volume of foreign currency exchanged in the state (or fees charged)

- percent of industry with membership in an active trade association

WORKFORCE TRANSITIONS

- percent of state workforce in import-intensive industries

- average length of unemployment for import-dislocated workers

- Research in *Iowa* revealed that an annual taxpayer expenditure of $700,000 for trade and investment development generated a return of $9.5 million in tax receipts. While export receipts were harder to document than investment-related receipts, exports nonetheless returned an estimated one-fifth of the total, or about $2 million each year.[81]

- In *Washington*, the Pacific Northwest Export Assistance Project created an estimated 166 new jobs in small firms (most in distressed communities) from export sales it arranged between March 1992 and December 1993. The personal income tax earnings from these new jobs alone yielded the state an estimated $330,000 per year, on a budget of $380,000—nearly break-even, even without including the savings realized by taking displaced timber workers off the unemployment rolls.[82]

- Firms under contract to *Oregon's* trade division generated new gross sales of $16 million on a budget of $3.5 million in the most recent biennium. "Our legislators are used to being presented huge, phony multipliers for state projects," says former Oregon trade director Glenn Ford, "but our numbers are real direct impacts."[83]

> The problem at the heart of American export promotion is not just the inadequacy of government programs— though these are legion— but the absence of a comprehensive, accessible trade-services *system*.

The Next Generation: Toward an International Development System

The problem at the heart of American export promotion is not just the inadequacy of government programs to help firms export—though the inadequacies are legion—but the absence of a comprehensive and accessible trade-services *system*, spanning both the public and private sectors, that serves the needs of existing and potential exporters. Such systems are long-established and well-developed in the economic structures of our international competitors.

Fundamental change in the way trade services are provided to industry will not originate in state trade offices alone. State trade directors

FIRST GENERATION

MISSION & GOALS

- job creation is the only goal
- focus only on generating exports
- promote just manufactured products

STRATEGIES AND SERVICE MIX

- focus on getting products represented overseas
- hawk off-the-shelf products for export
- work with the "export ready"
- services are homogenous
- help companies one-on-one
- clients get piecemeal services
- fees are used to supplement budgets
- regard foreigners only as potential customers
- target the foreign private sector

MEASURING SUCCESS

- maximize the number of office-sponsored events and participants
- gather client reports on immediate or expected export sales
- focus on export deals only
- survey program users
- gather testimonials

RELATIONSHIP TO STATE ECONOMIC-DEVELOPMENT MISSION

- programs collaborate through unstable turf agreements
- export budgets are fixed independently
- trade programs are on the periphery

RELATIONSHIP WITH PRIVATE SECTOR INSTITUTIONS & CLIENTS

- clients "take it or leave it"
- trade staff manage events
- novices can start just with government advice
- programs cope with meager export financing
- programs answer daily to elected officials

MISSION & GOALS

- competitiveness is an equally important goal
- focus on foreign market shares & strategic position
- promote high value-added services too

STRATEGIES AND SERVICE MIX

- develop trade relationships and "areas of influence"
- encourage market research and development of new products
- focus on building export readiness
- assistance is tailored to specific needs of the company
- assist industry associations or groups of firms
- clients receive holistic case management
- fees used as a strategic tool
- foreigners can be helpful teachers, motivators, partners
- consider foreign government contracts and major projects

MEASURING SUCCESS

- measure outcomes
- measure actual export deals over several years
- also monitor changes in firm capacity ("export readiness")
- survey all exporters
- use opinion surveys to attribute success and track changes over time

RELATIONSHIP TO STATE ECONOMIC DEVELOPMENT MISSION

- programs collaborate around measurable outcomes
- states develop a unified budget for international development
- trade is central to the state economic development mission

RELATIONSHIP WITH PRIVATE SECTOR INSTITUTIONS & CLIENTS

- clients participate in service design
- trade staff are "loaned executives"
- would-be exporters also need strong private advisors
- the banking system is brought into a dialogue over export financing
- programs answer daily to customers

Over the past fifteen years or so, a "first generation" state trade promotion and development capacity evolved through a sort of creeping incrementalism. Now a second—and fundamentally different—generation of effort is needed.

have neither the mandate nor the power individually to bring about wholesale reform, no matter how eager they may be to do so. The executive leadership of both the public and private sectors must be committed to the endeavor in order to forge deep working partnerships and secure needed resources.

Over the course of the last fifteen years or so, a "first generation" state trade promotion and development capacity evolved through a sort of creeping incrementalism—borrowing, adapting, responding to pressures, mandates, even customers. Now a second generation of effort is needed and, in some instances, is already developing. There are fundamental differences between the two generations, in objectives, relationships, funding, outputs and operational philosophy. *(See Figure 11.)*

But even the creation of an integrated trade-services system does not internationalize a state. To reach that larger objective, states need a capacity for managing their own foreign affairs and a civic capacity to support internationalization throughout the state. These final two components are covered in the ensuing chapters.

CHAPTER 5: BUILDING A STATE FOREIGN AFFAIRS CAPACITY

After perhaps a century of quiescence, state and local officials are returning to active duty in foreign policy. In the federal system, the national government retains ultimate control over formal treaties and matters of war, but it is not uncommon for state and local officials to meet foreign heads of state, collect and donate aid to troubled regions of the world, actively push for a particular change in U.S. foreign policy, or pursue unique commercial or cultural relationships with selected areas of the world.

Indeed, the Constitution places few restrictions on state engagement in foreign affairs and was intended to give states a central role in foreign policy, via their representation in the U.S. Senate. Some interpretations of the Constitution argue that individual states were intended to be directly engaged in foreign policy with the national government supervising, and only rarely forbidding, such actions.[84] As it has worked out, states are now probably much less active in foreign affairs than was originally envisioned, and the federal government much less attentive to what the states are doing.

Despite the growing importance of achieving global economic competitiveness, the daily grind of state and local governance has been so consuming that the average official has seen little reason to acquire an expertise in foreign relations, or to explore ways to professionalize a state's management of them.

Until now.

> No state can today ignore its involvement in global politics, relationships and institutions.

The Call for a State Foreign Policy

Five factors are pushing state and big-city governments to recognize and better organize their involvement in global politics, relationships and institutions.

THE INTERNATIONAL STATE: CRAFTING A STATEWIDE TRADE DEVELOPMENT SYSTEM

1. STATE "TURF" IS BEING INVADED

State and local jurisdictions traditionally have shaped policy in many areas important to economic development: banking, insurance, business subsidies, environmental regulations, highway safety and government procurement. But now these policies are affected by the North American Free Trade Agreement (NAFTA) and the General Agreement on Tariffs and Trade (GATT). Such issues are brought to international bargaining tables during negotiations because global trade has grown considerably over the decades, and because there is a new willingness around the world to view regulations that are based on local social values as potentially unfair barriers to trade.

Debates concerning these issues can get quite messy. For instance, Washington apple growers long fought for entry to the Japanese market but the Japanese resisted, citing allegations that a fumigant used on the Washington apples violated the Montreal protocol on the reduction of ozone-layer depleting substances.[85] The United States, in turn, has many value-based import restrictions, such as a new protocol requiring imported Mexican heifers to be treated with specified anesthetic and suture procedures during spaying.[86]

> Economic policies traditionally shaped by state and local jurisdictions now may be affected by NAFTA and GATT.

Deep differences in cultural interpretations of health, safety and ethics ensure that the trade negotiations and agreements will remain highly controversial. These issues get even stickier since state and local governments have no real standing in international dispute-resolution procedures. The U.S. federal government is the only recognized party to a complaint over state actions; and it must respond to a negative ruling by compensating the injured country or, in the worst case, by overriding the state law.

Thus, although the NAFTA and GATT treaties have been signed, the states' involvement is really just beginning. For one thing, the U.S. trade representative has requested states to identify laws, regulations, programs and policies that may be inconsistent with obligations under various international agreements. Some may be "grandfathered in." Others may not, in which case states will have to bring their laws into compliance.

Inevitably, some states, with the federal government representing them, will have to defend certain policies in an international court. A state's ability to defend its policies will depend on careful documentation of legislative "intent" and of the beneficiaries of the measure in question—information few states are currently able to provide.

One example of states rising to this new challenge is the Western Governors' Association's work toward a multistate initiative to develop an ongoing capacity for managing state sovereignty issues, such as international legal threats to the West's relatively tough environmental regulations.

2. FOREIGN RELATIONSHIPS ARE PART OF EXPORT DEVELOPMENT

In most places around the world, trade is the ultimate insider's game. Culture and pragmatism impel businesspeople to reduce the risk involved in pursuing trade and to maximize the potential for follow-up deals by working through friends and long-trusted business associates. Although some U.S. exporters obtain good results through advertising or by picking an agent off a list, many export deals—particularly those involving major projects like hospitals or power plants—must be jointly identified and developed through a long-term process of building trust, familiarity and personal networks.

> **Export deals depend on a long-term process of building trust, familiarity and personal networks.**

Sister Cities International has embraced this concept, and other groups are also beginning to invest in creating long-term foreign relationships between states or communities in this country and similar jurisdictions in other nations. One example is the Red River Corridor project, which involves parts of Minnesota, North Dakota and the province of Manitoba that lie within the Red River basin. Besides crossing a national boundary at its own inception, this grassroots initiative is designed to bridge the Atlantic by linking people and businesses in the Corridor with those in the French region of Brittany, through a broad array of business and cultural relationships. The program's leaders anticipate that the economic and cultural similarities of the two regions will foster the identification of trade deals, both between the two regions and with similarly configured regions elsewhere in the world.

FLORIDA ASSOCIATION OF VOLUNTARY AGENCIES FOR CARIBBEAN ACTION, INC.

The Florida Association of Voluntary Agencies for Caribbean Action, Inc. (FAVA/CA) is a private, not-for-profit international development organization incorporated in 1982 to enhance trade, strengthen democracy and improve living conditions in the Caribbean. In 1986, FAVA/CA created the Florida International Volunteer Corps in response to increasing requests from the foreign aid community for quick-response, low-cost technical assistance and training in health, education, business and agriculture.

What distinguishes FAVA/CA's Corps from the Peace Corps or a Sister City program are its focus on small-scale technical problems with high-impact results and the short duration of its projects. It places skilled Floridian volunteers in projects that typically last an average of 11 days.

More than 300 FAVA/CA Volunteer Corps missions have served 14 nations of the Caribbean and Central America, training over 7,000 individuals. Four full-time and one half-time staff members—the total staff—recruit, screen, place and evaluate all volunteers. Corps volunteer-consultants may serve requesting governments or the private sector; they receive only travel and subsistence reimbursement for their work. A U.S. Agency for International Development (USAID) study found that Corps consultants can be provided to requesting nations at 40 to 50 percent of the cost of commercial technical assistance services.

The Volunteer Corps enjoys statutory authority and has received a state appropriation each year since 1986. In FY 1993, $121,606 in state funds comprised 18 percent of the total budget. Private funds, including cash donations and in-kind services, amounted to 47 percent of the budget. The balance was made up of federal grants and contracts. In short, FAVA/CA raises $5 for every dollar the state contributes. The state, sold on the wisdom of the approach, doubled its appropriation for 1994-95.

FAVA/CA projects make the host country's business community more likely to sit up and take positive notice of Florida and its citizens. That's partly because more than half the FAVA/CA projects are income-producing, raising the level of purchasing power in the Caribbean community and the prospects for trade. Florida volunteers, for example, taught instructors at a St. Vincent woodworking center how to make beehives, and then instructed the community's agricultural leaders on how to get double duty out of the bees by using them as crop pollinators.

Other FAVA/CA training projects, such as emergency-medical staff training, sickle cell awareness programs, sports development, and drug abuse prevention, are geared toward improving health and living standards. These activities produce goodwill, goodwill promotes trust, and trust generates business opportunities for the state. The Florida Department of Commerce has included the FAVA/CA team on trade missions to the Caribbean.

3. IMMIGRATION, INTERNATIONAL TOURISM AND FOREIGN INVESTMENT INCREASINGLY RAISE TOUGH ISSUES— AND NEW OPPORTUNITIES

California's recent Proposition 187, which sought to limit immigrants' access to state-provided social services, and Florida's lawsuit to get the federal government to pay for social services delivered to illegal immigrants epitomize the tensions generated by the growing foreign presence in U.S. life.

Yet as immigration, international tourism and foreign investment grow in volume and importance, states are facing some new, tough and often dicey questions. For example:

■■ Should a state allow foreign companies to participate in a state-supported research effort?

■■ How should a state respond to the foreign purchase of a college?

States

**must find ways to
address tensions generated
by the growing foreign presence
in U.S. life.
They must also recognize and
utilize the opportunities
that presence brings.**

■■ What priority should teaching English-as-a-second-language (ESL) be given over other adult literacy goals?

■■ How should a locality deal with a golf club that excludes foreigners?

■■ What about cultural clashes between long-time residents and recent immigrants or refugees?

An increasing foreign presence also offers states new opportunities. Foreign tourists and students, for instance, represent potential export earnings; some states have even considered recruiting foreign students with offers of education loans.

4. STATES AND CIVIC GROUPS ARE INCREASINGLY ACTIVE IN GLOBAL HUMANITARIAN PROJECTS

The growing people-to-people involvement in democratization movements around the world and in peace and environmental issues fosters grassroots diplomacy. Constituents increasingly call upon state and local leaders to address humanitarian causes.

Many states, for example, rushed forward with pledges of aid and technical assistance to Eastern Europe at the end of the Cold War. However, even though the National Governors' Association was supporting the states' involvement, much of the aid activity was ad hoc and sporadic. The recipient countries lost patience with the unpredictability of the aid and the lack of a consultative process for setting aid priorities.[87]

> If states are to gain respect and standing in the foreign aid arena, they must better focus and coordinate their missions.

If states are to gain respect and standing in the foreign aid arena, they must better focus and coordinate their missions. Florida's long-running aid initiative in the Caribbean, FAVA/CA, for example, stands out as a particularly well-executed mission, and one that blends aid with long-term trade objectives. *(See "Florida Association of Voluntary Agencies for Caribbean Action, Inc.," on page 108.)*

5. FOREIGN INSTITUTIONS ARE A GROWING SOURCE OF INFORMATION, CONTACTS AND OTHER RESOURCES

In tight fiscal times, states and businesses must look beyond the federal government for support and ideas. With the rise in visibility and activity of international institutions, and the increasing ease of access and speed of exchange brought on by telecommunications options like the Internet, states—as well as their agencies, their localities and their citizens—have somewhere to turn.

The United Nations, for instance, has 16 specialized subunits and numerous voluntary organizations, each of which offers access to data and contacts that could be useful to state and local governments on issues ranging from AIDS to crime control. Columbus, Ohio sought and won the right to become one of 21 initial sites worldwide for a United Nations project using computers and communications technology to speed trade by eliminating paperwork. The Ohio "infoport," now known as TradePoint USA, is the first one in North America, and is expected to stimulate the development of trade in the surrounding region.[88]

> **In tight fiscal times, states and businesses must look beyond our own borders for support and ideas.**

In addition, multilateral lending institutions, such as the Inter-American Development Bank (IDB), provide project financing and wield considerable commercial influence in the regions they serve. States can help businesses contact these institutions and maintain lines of communication.

Building a State Foreign Policy Infrastructure

Increasingly then, the issue is not *whether* state and local governments should pursue direct contact with foreign governments and their institutions, but rather *how* to develop consistent and professional policies, programs and relationships that are fully integrated into a state's larger economic development strategy.

To protect and expand its long-term economic interests, a truly "internationalized" state might:

In 1987, Dallas created a Commission on International Development to address the global economic and social forces affecting the city. The commission's principal accomplishment was broadening the scope of the city's Office of International Affairs (OIA), which had been established in 1981 as the Office of Protocol to meet the city's responsibilities in hosting foreign dignitaries.

MISSION AND ORGANIZATION

With a mandate from the Commission to add international business development and other functions, OIA began rapidly to evolve into a municipal "foreign ministry." OIA is charged with:

- promoting the expansion of international trade and foreign investment in Dallas, the development of the city's international economic infrastructure, and improvements in international air service

- supporting cultural, educational, scientific and other international exchanges, including sister-city programs, and relating them to opportunities for new business ties and economic growth

- marketing Dallas internationally through programs and hospitality for distinguished foreign visitors, and through foreign travel to promote the city's economic and other international interests

- helping attract international exhibitions, sports events, conventions and tourism to Dallas

- serving as the city's focal point for contacts with foreign government representatives, international organizations and immigrant communities

The present OIA staff works out of city hall and consists of a director, three other professionals—for protocol, business and special events—and two secretaries. The staff is supplemented by a corps of 50 volunteers, who assist with protocol functions.

OIA relies on $265,000 in city funds to pay salaries and benefits for the OIA staff. The remainder of its operating budget ($135,000 in 1992-93) is raised privately through the annual Dallas Ambassadors Forum, an affair that brings 40 to 50 foreign ambassadors to Dallas for a weekend of social events and presentations on Dallas' business climate. The event yields about $500,000 yearly.

Because the non-personnel portion of its operating budget comes entirely from these private funds, OIA enjoys considerably greater flexibility than do typical city government offices. For example, in Dallas, even if funds were available in the regular city budget, it would not be politically possible to use taxpayers' money to entertain foreign dignitaries and pay for the mayor's foreign travel.

RESULTS: ALL OVER THE MAP

The record of OIA shows that deliberate effort to promote internationalization can pay dividends. Since 1989, OIA has:

- launched an initiative to position Dallas as the economic hub of the North American Free Trade Area

- enhanced Dallas' image as an international business center by promoting the establishment of the French-supported International School of Dallas— which makes the city more competitive in attracting European investment

- facilitated the opening of 11 new consular, trade and other foreign government offices

- helped launch two new international air routes

- recruited Dallasites living abroad to promote the city on a voluntary basis

- helped establish new sister-city relationships with Riga, Latvia; Brno, Czech Republic; Monterey, Mexico and Sendai, Japan

- organized the visits of six chiefs of state, including Queen Elizabeth, and 55 visits by foreign cabinet-level officials

- supported cultural activities, such as the staging of international exhibits and the city's successful bid for the 1994 World Cup

These activities, as well as knowledgeable responses to specific inquiries, have enhanced connections with potential foreign customers, investors and business partners.

- create an institutional structure that scans foreign policy developments that might affect the state, and facilitates an appropriate response;

- establish a clear identity with foreigners;

- cultivate "areas of influence" with strategic foreign markets by investing deeply in business and diplomatic relationships in those places;

- participate in federal-level advisory groups, such as the U.S. Trade Representative's Intergovernmental Policy Advisory Committee or the State and Local Working Group of the federal government's Trade Program Coordinating Committee;

Increasingly, the issue is not *whether* state and local governments should pursue direct contact with foreign governments and their institutions, but *how*.

- take advantage of information resources of the United Nations and other international organizations; and

- fully utilize the many federal and foundation resources available to support international trade, education and cultural understanding.

Dallas, which already has an Office of International Affairs, provides one model for systematic foreign policy management by a locality. *(See "Dallas: A City Office of International Affairs," page 112.)*

Overall, states need a coherent foreign policy framework in which competing interests can be weighed and prioritized. Officials might implement professional foreign policy management by using a number of strategies, described briefly below.

1. DEVELOP AN "INTELLIGENCE CENTER" FOR INTERNATIONAL DEVELOPMENTS

Critical industry trends and international phenomena—like "lean production," *perestroika*, EC 1992, ISO 9000 and NAFTA—were all on the

THE GATT PROCUREMENT CODE:
A MUDDLED STATE RESPONSE

The GATT Procurement Code requires national governments that signed the agreement—called the *signatories*—to operate goods- and services-procurement programs. By thus prohibiting favoritism toward local bidders, the new code provides exporters access to billions of dollars in government procurement contracts worldwide.

The Procurement Code negotiated in the 1960s during the Tokyo Round of GATT talks covered central—that is, national-level—government purchases of most goods above a contract value of $172,000. The negotiators under the recent Uruguay Round expanded the code's coverage to encompass subnational government purchases.

In the Uruguay Round talks, whereas other countries could negotiate with confidence on behalf of their subnational governments, the United States felt compelled to consult state governments and solicit their explicit pledge to open their procurement procedures. In mid-1991, the U.S. Trade Representative sent a letter to all governors requesting their input and pledges to open up at least certain aspects of their procurement systems.

Very few states responded to that letter, largely because they weren't prepared with a coherent system to deal with all the issues it raised. Some letters bounced between the state trade and procurement offices. Other letters gathered dust while legislatures were out of session, since legislative approval was essential to making any firm commitment. Still other letters went unanswered due to troublesome technical questions—such as the mechanics of advertising RFPs internationally—and concerns that labor unions might object to increased foreign competition.

After months of one-on-one prodding, the U.S. negotiators finally got a majority of U.S. states to write a letter of support. Many state letters offered vague commitments, however, and the foreign negotiators challenged the U.S. assertion that they had the commitments they needed.[90]

The states and the Office of the U.S. Trade Representative are now attempting to improve communication through the identification of fixed "points of contact" within each governor's administration.

radar screen of internationalists years before the vast majority of state and local officials started developing responses to them. States need the capacity to anticipate and alert leaders to troubles as well as opportunities spawned by international developments. Without a central vision of the state's role in the international economy, state policies develop piecemeal—and often conflict with each other.

> **W**ithout a central vision of the state's role in the international economy, state policies develop piecemeal—and often conflict with each other.

One example of the need for an "intelligence center" can be found in the sluggishness of most states' response to the issues raised during the early stages of the GATT negotiations. *(See "The GATT Procurement Code: A Muddled State Response," previous page.)* Hawaii, Florida and California have perhaps demonstrated the deepest commitments to building foreign policy capacities in the governors' offices. *(See "Hawaii's Office of International Relations," on page 118.)* And Kentucky has what is probably the most advanced legislative capacity for tracking the local impact of foreign policy trends and institutions. *(See "Kentucky's Office of Federal and International Relations" on page 120.)*

2. MAINTAIN A DIRECTORY OF CURRENT AND FORMER RESIDENT "EXPERTS"

Internationally active academics, business executives, community organizers, foreign students and others can be valuable assets in a state's search for understanding and contacts in key foreign markets. These individuals might be catalogued, on a voluntary basis, and made part of a permanent "international experts" network.

Similarly, former residents who have moved elsewhere often retain family or emotional ties to states and communities where they grew up or worked in prior years. Former residents who have risen to influential positions in federal and international organizations should be catalogued, where possible, and invited back as guest speakers or in other roles to share their knowledge and contacts. The same concept would apply to foreign graduates of state institutions.

3. TRAIN LEADERS IN BASIC TRADE POLICY AND STATE TRADE HISTORY

Kentucky State Senator John "Eck" Rose observes an important, growing trend: "Today, many foreign delegations, both governmental and business, often circumvent America's traditional center of financial power, New York City, or the center of federal power, Washington, D.C., and deal directly with state or local governmental units or private sector business." Yet as state and local leaders increasingly come into contact with foreigners, their limited knowledge of trade and commercial history, much less protocol, sometimes puts them at a disadvantage. Foreigners typically have a profound and emotional view of their country's commercial and political relationship with the United States, a viewpoint that American leaders may not appreciate, much less be prepared to debate. Moreover, Americans rarely have a similarly developed view of our relationship with other nations.

One way of overcoming these barriers is through a tailored training program. In a 1992 survey by the National Association of State Development Agencies (NASDA), 14 trade offices said they offer some form of trade development training for elected officials. One option for those who don't might be to internationalize the existing training curricula for newly elected officials, or to commission training from other institutions, such as universities, world trade centers or local trade programs.

Nebraska offers one example of a state initiative specifically designed to educate community leaders about the transition to a global economy. The Nebraska Global Communities project, which involves a handbook and seminars, offers a tailored approach to getting local leaders up to speed on global competition.

> Internationally active academics, organizers, businesspeople and students can be valuable assets in a state's search for understanding and contacts in key foreign markets.

State and local leaders might also be encouraged to go abroad on foundation-supported study tours. Former Iowa state representative Thomas E. Swartz supports this concept, "Global pressures today require state lawmakers to make decisions influencing the competitiveness of their state's businesses. It is only fitting that [we] gain firsthand experience of the competitive world around us."

Hawaii exports very little in the form of manufactured products, yet its ethnic heritage, island status, geographic location and economic dependence on agriculture exports, the defense industry and international tourism have impelled it to take its foreign relationships more seriously than many other states. As a result, cultural exchange, international education and the state's global identity are considered equally important to export promotion.

In 1989, Gov. John Waihee created Hawaii's Office of International Relations (OIR) to coordinate the state's international activities. OIR started with a budget of $650,000, enough to support a staff of five policy researchers, who helped conduct an initial statewide, grassroots strategic planning process.

The resulting plan produced the following objectives for OIR:

- Develop comprehensive international policies and priorities for the state, such as sister-state agreements and protocol matters, and coordinate state policy on international environment, trade and health issues affecting Hawaii.

- Analyze appropriate international issues and opportunities by supplying clear, pertinent information on trade negotiations, international political developments and business opportunities that can have a significant impact on Hawaii's economic future.

- Educate the media to present an accurate and positive portrayal of Hawaii's economic climate.

- Further improve business conditions and attract clean industries such as higher education, health and telecommunications.

- Help develop Hawaiian science and technology industries by assisting with the international aspects of state and private efforts regarding new technologies. This includes capital attraction, facilitating state access to international networks, and advancing translation services.

- Help advance the internationalization of Hawaii through education to increase the worldwide attraction of Hawaii as a "Geneva of the Pacific," regional headquarters for international firms, and a conference site.

The OIR lasted for five years with a staff of up to ten people. But budgetary pressures and the drive to streamline government led newly elected Governor Ben Cayetano to close the shop in December 1994.

Even so, Governor Cayetano still supports the core concept of the OIR. That support, and the legislature's sense of ownership of the office (it was a statutory entity), may permit its return in some form once budgetary pressures lessen.

Meanwhile, Brenda Foster, OIR's director at the time it closed, continues to manage international relations for the state's executive branch. Ms. Foster is pursuing a strategy of building teams within different departments to help her carry out the state's international objectives.

4. BUILD A POSITIVE IMAGE WITH FOREIGN STUDENTS AND VISITORS

Foreign tourists, businesspeople, scholars and students often represent the middle class and political elite of their home countries. Making their visits easier can have important long-term economic and even political benefits. But achieving such benefits requires assessing and improving how visiting foreigners perceive the state's image.

Most states have a formal international visitors program that can help with such an assessment. These programs range from the relatively well-known Council for International Visitors (CIV) organizations to the quiet efforts of Rotary Club International. Indeed, CIV's non-profit, volunteer organizations in 102 U.S. locations serve as the domestic "field staff" for the U.S. Information Agency's well-regarded international visitor's program.

Unfortunately, considering the potential importance international visitors hold for future business dealings,

State and local leaders can gain knowledge of trade and commercial history and protocol through tailored training programs and foundation-supported study tours.

KENTUCKY'S OFFICE OF FEDERAL AND INTERNATIONAL RELATIONS

State legislatures generally have lagged behind executive branches in their international policy capacity and involvement. So the Kentucky Legislature was a pioneer when it established a legislative "brain center" for tracking and responding to international challenges and opportunities.

In Kentucky, both houses of the Legislature share a single research office—the Kentucky Legislative Research Commission (KLRC). Although the KLRC had been involved in international issues for more than a decade, in 1991 it sought to formalize a process to identify and satisfy legislators' international information needs.

In doing so, the KLRC recognized the changes taking place not just in the role of state legislators, but in the type of problems they must address. Issues like drug abuse and health concerns can now involve—and may require—international joint action, data sharing, or the exchange of ideas and best-practice information.

By networking with external organizations like the United Nations and the Organization for Economic Cooperation and Development, the KLRC hoped to develop new information resources to support the work of *all* legislative committees—not just those that deal with trade, natural resources and agriculture—and to enable legislators to respond directly to observable international change and opportunity.

Therefore, the Kentucky Legislature created the Office of Federal and International Relations (OFIR). Its mission is "to assist the Kentucky General Assembly and legislative staff to develop the capacity and infrastructure to deal effectively and efficiently with national and international issues that impact the citizens of the Commonwealth of Kentucky." OFIR was created by administrative action as a part of KLRC, with no additional funding.

OFIR seeks to:

- welcome foreign delegations and provide them with specific orientation programs on Kentucky and its legislative process

- serve as a clearinghouse for international data and information that complements what the legislative committees already collect

- form liaisons with traditional and nontraditional local, national and international entities, such as Sister Cities International, the United Nations and others

- coordinate with the U.S. State Department, Congress and other federal agencies and organizations

- monitor major federal executive-agency regulations and congressional legislation, such as that dealing with foreign-language training, that will have a direct impact upon the Commonwealth of Kentucky

- develop a clearinghouse to receive and distribute relevant federal information, such as reports from the U.S. International Trade Commission, to state legislators and legislative committees

- offer translation and interpretation services for official communications involving legislators

- provide technical assistance to legislators, including drafting resolutions on international issues

- prepare cultural background papers on foreign countries and develop briefing sessions on emerging international issues

- coordinate with the governor's office and executive agencies

OFIR also produces a quarterly newsletter, *Kentucky's Global Connections*, which is distributed to roughly 4,000 legislators and other Kentucky leaders. The newsletter covers the widest possible range of international topics, including events occurring in Kentucky, international issues that affect or involve Kentuckians, statistics and references.

The KLRC Office of Federal and International Relations and its work have been well received by both the legislative and executive branches. By working closely with other international entities in the state, such as the International Visitors Council and state agencies, the office has helped advance a number of causes, including a major push by the state to become a visible player in the global environmental protection movement.

many states pay little attention to such organizations. State agencies and other trade organizations often host important delegations without any awareness of the resources and contacts available from established visitors' programs.

Stronger relationships between state trade agencies and established visitors' programs these groups would be both mutually beneficial and catalytic.

Stronger relationships between these groups could be both mutually beneficial and catalytic. Closer relationships with state trade programs would help the state's CIVs, for instance, "market" themselves to the U.S. Information Agency—which they must do to get their share of visitors—or write grant proposals to foundations or corporations for operational support. Closer relationships would also help visitor programs identify the appropriate state and local business and government leaders to meet with their guests. This task is especially difficult when the staff and volunteers who set up the appointments have limited knowledge of the region's changing business profile, or are asked to arrange visits to rural settings outside their normal service range.

5. IDENTIFY AND SUPPORT RESIDENT ETHNIC ENCLAVES

Recent immigrants and strong ethnic communities offer a wealth of business and government contacts, language and cultural skills, knowledge of business practices, and a vast reservoir of goodwill and commitment to improving the lot of both countries.

New Jersey has embraced the concept of linking immigrant communities with trade goals. East Orange, for example, has a high concentration of African immigrants, including some 2,000 immigrants from Ghana. In September 1993, the city and a group of Ghanaian immigrants organized a two-week trade mission that included state and local government officials. The 44 members of the delegation met with Ghana's president and business leaders, and left with a fistful of deals and leads. After the trip, New Jersey's director of the Division of International Trade, Phil Ferzan, commented, "One lesson is that ethnic groups can bring a lot to the table, and they will do so for the love of their native countries as well as the United States."[91]

Global economic and political forces affect every facet of state activity. The executive and legislative branches of state government, together with the administrative and policy units of local government, must access intelligence about the world around them—and act on it—if they are to compete effectively.

But ultimately, the foundations for trade and global competitiveness must go deeper than the trade and business leadership of a state. Top decisionmakers are not the only ones in need of better intelligence about the changing global economy. Today's youth and workers will require a higher level of international skill than most currently attain if they are to succeed in an increasingly international business environment. Voters, too, need information and learning opportunities to better understand the nature of the global economy and the growing presence of foreigners in their daily lives, if they are to choose wisely among leaders and policy options. The next chapter turns to this challenge.

> **U**ltimately, the foundations for trade and global competitiveness must go deeper than the trade and business leadership of a state. Today's youth...workers...voters... *all* need to better understand the global economy and its presence in their daily lives.

Trade is not a spectator sport. An international state must draw on the energies not just of its active exporters, but also its suppliers, workforce, local leaders and even the general public. Apathy, much less resistance, can damage the trade prospects of exporters and the competitive position of the region and state.

In the matter of internationalization, the United States is, in a sense, a victim of its own success and of an accident of geography. With our huge domestic economy and oceans isolating us from much of the rest of the world, the United States has, until quite recently, had little need to know, appreciate or understand the languages, people or cultures of other countries. Even now, there is an undercurrent of xenophobia in public debate on issues ranging from welfare reform to foreign aid. As an American World Bank official intimated a few years ago to an audience of southern state policy leaders: The U.S. public is in the process of "rediscovering" a global interdependence that was always there, and it may be doing so with a level of ignorance and arrogance that could damage business or foreign relations.[92]

> An international state must draw on the energies not just of its active exporters, but also its suppliers, workforce, local leaders and even the general public. Apathy, much less resistance, can damage trade prospects.

Many private sector leaders agree. At a 1993 national conference designed to provide private sector and state government input into the design of the first National Export Strategy, business executives strongly urged the government to give priority to the creation of a public trade mentality.[93] At the time of the conference, passage of NAFTA was in serious doubt, and efforts to lift U.S. prohibitions against trade with Vietnam had been repeatedly rebuffed. In the view of the business executives and others present, the public did not have sufficient information to make rational choices with respect to trade policy.

Likewise, following the close vote on NAFTA, shocked officials in the Office of the U.S. Trade Representative discussed forming a public trade

Because their international experience is shallow and their suspicions deep, persuading the general public of the need to inform themselves about other cultures and the global economy will require sustained dialogue.

education campaign. Newspaper inserts and lobby displays aimed at schoolchildren would, it was hoped, help raise awareness about the global economy.

Although a commendable concept, such an effort is probably too small in scope and insufficiently neutral in appearance to reach voters. The sensationalized debate over NAFTA *was*, at least in part, a product of this country's economic illiteracy, but it was also the bitter harvest of decades of growing public mistrust of authority. Isolated messages on trade packaged as "infomercials" are unlikely to change that. Reaching voters will require sustained dialogue, because the international experience base of the general public—and even that of top opinion leaders—is too limited, and their suspicions too deep, to be overcome through sporadic or passive communication.

Identifying Local-International Links

Although well-informed people can and do disagree over trade policies, the soundness and consistency of decisions can only improve through greater international and economic literacy.

It is often at the personal level that average citizens are provided opportunities to truly comprehend a different culture. Thus, international education and outreach efforts work best at the local level. Opportunities for dialogue and long-term learning usually can be found close to home—in schools, the workplace, community networks and the media, and through local "experts" such as exporters, faculty, foreign students and others who have lived or worked abroad.

THE ROLE OF GRASSROOTS LINKAGES

How do people learn about other nations and peoples? Media reports, tourist visits, and casual contact with recent immigrants may reveal something about other cultures' behaviors, customs and history. They convey less, however, about beliefs, values, assumptions and thought processes—the central but often less visible features that define a culture. It is through nontourist trips abroad and through serving as hosts for foreign visitors that average citizens gain the most meaningful exposure to foreigners and foreign cultures. [94]

The task before state leaders now is to cultivate local culture and local friendship linkages as potential assets for trade development. One of the best routes for promoting this exposure is through internationally active civic clubs and organizations. Cities, towns and civic groups are increasingly active overseas, some even surpassing states in their level of involvement in trade and cultural exchange.

> The task before state leaders now is to cultivate local culture and local friendship linkages as potential assets for trade development.

Too frequently, however, state programs ignore this grassroots international leadership, failing to see the potential trade gains. The Red River Trade Corridor, discussed earlier, is one example of such a grassroots initiative. Community and business organizations in the Corridor are pairing up with French counterparts of a similar economic base to learn more about each other before embarking on some joint ventures.

Similarly, the Sister Cities International program has recently embraced trade development as an important goal of city partnerships. It is no coincidence that Oregon—home to the giant athletic-wear corporation Nike—has a Sister City relationship with the athletic footwear capital of China, or that Napa Valley, California, is paired with the famous wine-growing region of (the former Soviet) Georgia.

Some state and local leaders deploy their cultural assets to help attract foreign interest and investors. The Greater Philadelphia International Network, for instance, supports the international tours of the Greater Philadelphia Orchestra for that express purpose.[95]

THE ROLE OF THE MEDIA

The media are among the most pervasive and powerful educators of adults, but their coverage of international affairs is often limited to sound

With occasional exceptions, local media coverage of foreign economic issues that affect a state or locality typically is limited and weak.

bites and headlines, mostly about natural and political disasters. Even our major national newspapers, like *The New York Times* or *Wall Street Journal*, are not as cosmopolitan in their coverage of events, or in the diversity of viewpoints, as some of their counterparts in Europe and elsewhere.

With occasional exceptions, local media coverage of foreign economic issues that affect a state or locality typically is limited and weak. In a May 1993 survey of state and local trade advocates conducted by the Clearinghouse on State International Policies, only 12 percent gave a better than "fair" rating to local media coverage of such international issues.[96] This finding was echoed in a 1993 European Community survey of U.S. state organizations. When asked about the quality of local media coverage of Europe, most state officials reported their media to be "useless."[97]

One reason for the poor ratings is that media organizations are rarely structured to tell the story of how rapid globalization affects local economies. The national media and a handful of major metropolitan newspapers do have foreign bureaus, but their overseas reporters are focused on the progress of foreign events, not on how such political, social and business developments might affect state and local issues covered by the paper back home.

More often, it is *not* the foreign correspondent, but rather political, city and business reporters and their editors who influence public perceptions of trade and of foreigners in the community. Many local reporters, products of the same education system as their audience, lack the depth of understanding of global economics or the appreciation of different cultures necessary to handle the subject matter more than superficially.

Relations between trade offices and the media can be particularly difficult, adding to the problem. As noted earlier, the media frequently portray international travel by state or local officials as junketeering. This has the direct effect of chilling officials' travel—which in turn sharply curtails not just trade officials' own understanding of the state's needs in the swiftly changing global environment but, obviously, their ability to communicate what understanding they *do* have to the media.

In the Clearinghouse's survey, only 40 percent of the trade advocates rated the local media as "supportive" of trade development efforts. Trade officials believe that, when it comes to the media, substantive questions may not get asked without prompting, and efforts to educate reporters and editors may go unrewarded.

THE ROLE OF INTERNATIONAL EDUCATION

In 1986, Virginia Gov. Gerald L. Baliles urged his fellow southern governors and other policy leaders to reintroduce language, culture and geography training into the schools. Baliles, then chair of the Southern Governors' Association, was firmly committed to growth through trade, and had observed with rising concern that the next generation was graduating from school unprepared for global competition.

Baliles' plea for international education drew from a report, *International Education: Cornerstone to Competition*, produced by the blue-ribbon Advisory Council on International Education.[98] Today, the international education community regards the release of the *Cornerstone* report as a watershed. As a result of this and other efforts, geography and languages were reintroduced in some schools, and not just in the South.

THE LANGUAGE BARRIER. Still, more remains to be done. Only 7.6 percent of U.S. elementary schoolchildren in the 1992-93 academic year received any kind of foreign-language instruction. Yet among America's international competitors—in Europe, for example—that figure approaches 100 percent.

In today's work environment, knowing a foreign language is already both a blue- and white-collar work requirement.

Foreign languages continue to languish in this country. In a world where English is the generally accepted language of international commerce and business management instruction, foreign-language training often is dismissed as unnecessary and expensive. It is argued, for instance, that only a tiny proportion of students ever make use of their foreign-language training. Yet this limited view fails to recognize that:

■■ translators cannot convey the full meaning of a complex interaction, nor are they appropriate in the social settings that form business trust and lead to deal-making

■■ learning a language also teaches cultural understanding

■■ once one foreign language is learned, another can be more readily acquired

■■ just like science and math courses, language training teaches critical thinking skills and lays the foundation for acquisition of advanced skills

■■ there is evidence that language training is correlated with higher academic achievement and improved cognitive capacity among youngsters[99]

In 1992-93, only 7.6 percent of U.S. elementary schoolchildren received any kind of foreign-language instruction. Among America's international competitors— in Europe, for example—that figure approaches 100 percent.

But most important, in today's work environment, knowing a foreign language is already both a blue- and white-collar work requirement. From hospital pediatric wards to courts, food stores, tourist attractions, trucking and architecture companies, non-English-speaking people are the customers, proprietors, workforce and business partners of companies and institutions based in the United States.

Besides souring the public on the emergence of an international economy, foreign-language and cultural barriers threaten to dampen both trade *and* productivity. Sara Garretson, the executive director of the New York Industrial Technology Assistance Corporation (ITAC), is convinced that poor communication is a seriously underestimated barrier to industrial modernization.[100] In one instance, ITAC staff found that translations through a sequence of six different languages were needed to establish communication between a sewing machine operator who was performing a task incorrectly and the supervisor who gave the original instructions. In short, in today's economy, homogenous workforces will increasingly be the exception, not the rule.

THE CULTURE BARRIER. Cultural sensitivity and understanding also are important for interpreting and anticipating a customer's or supplier's business decisions. Accepted business practices vary from country to country, even within western industrialized nations. Differences in business law, accounting, entertainment and ethics can present confusing and misleading signals to an outsider. This intimidates U.S. businesses. Indeed, senior-level employees of major corporations frequently are said to lack the confidence to approach even *U.S.-based* foreign businesses.[101]

Cultural skills are required of the entire workforce, not just executives. As more managers delegate more production decisions to front-line workers, and as customers are encouraged to speak directly with workers, blue-collar America must cope with the increasingly foreign profile of the customer base, workforce, corporate ownership and competitors. This is doubly true of retail and other service operations, where workers are in close contact with an increasingly international public.

> **A**s the customer base, workforce, corporate ownership and competition take on an increasingly foreign profile, cultural skills are required not just of executives but of the entire workforce.

Building Civic International Literacy

Communities are a logical focal point for efforts to educate and engage the American public in international matters. State leaders might work with, or at least support, existing international experts and advocates in local institutions—for example, schools, media, churches and city hall—to establish:

■■ sustained community involvement in overseas business, charitable and cultural initiatives

■■ routine contact between isolated business communities and foreign business delegations coming through the state

- peer contact between foreigners and all strata of citizens

- fully internationalized curricula and student life

- ongoing international education in the workplace

- voter understanding of and support for global economic integration

States might begin with an assessment of how well these objectives are already being met and where progress still needs to be made. State policymakers could follow any number of strategies for building a civic capacity around trade, but some specific programs and activities that might be particularly useful are described below.

1. PROMOTE BETTER USE OF AVAILABLE INTERNATIONAL RESOURCES

At a minimum, state and local leaders might take better advantage of the civic resources they have—foreign students, scholars and visitors, as well as established ethnic leaders in the community. For instance, visiting foreign business and government representatives might be invited to meet with local editorial boards, school officials, vocational classes, civic clubs, community centers and a variety of businesses. Foreign students, too, may describe their home countries to schoolchildren and participate in special events.

> At a minimum, state and local leaders might take better advantage of the civic resources they have—foreign students, scholars, visitors and established ethnic leaders in the community.

2. SUPPORT LOCAL-INTERNATIONAL CIVIC EXCHANGES

Most cities have "gone it alone" into Sister City programs and other activities. States might explore ways to encourage local participation in foreign affairs, even if only to lend credibility, staff expertise and contacts. States might discover that cities will, in turn, have much to offer, such as increased visibility abroad, door-opening contacts, trade leads, and access to information that might support the state's foreign policy interests.

International contact and exchange requires resources, however, and poor communities will rarely get involved with foreign cultures without financial and other assistance. To begin with, the protocol for hosting a foreign delegation requires the host to cover many, if not all, expenses incurred locally. Further, the host community almost always will receive an invitation to visit the guests in their homeland. Rural and minority communities may need special help identifying corporate support and assistance in preparing for the protocol aspects of exchanges.

3. SUPPORT CIVIC INVOLVEMENT IN CHARITABLE ACTIVITIES ABROAD

States, cities and civic groups already are active in charitable projects abroad. Donors can grow frustrated by their limited ability to deliver on promises or supply the full range of aid that is required. States might explore the advantages of coordinating and facilitating aid directed to important emerging markets. For example, Florida officials have supported targeted foreign aid and recognized the value of such aid in building future trade relationships. *(See "Florida Association of Voluntary Agencies for Caribbean Action, Inc," page 108.)*

> **S**tates might explore the advantages of coordinating and facilitating aid directed to important emerging markets.

4. ENCOURAGE LOCAL MEDIA COVERAGE OF FOREIGN ECONOMIC AND CULTURAL AFFAIRS

When it comes to trade, the media are important vehicles for raising awareness and changing public attitudes. The task can be made easier by engaging the media in a sustained and informal dialogue involving other stakeholders, such as exporters and academic leaders, and focusing on activities that make it easier for the media to cover the local angle on international issues.[102]

5. PROMOTE WORKPLACE TRAINING IN GLOBAL AFFAIRS

The workplace is another logical place to focus a campaign to educate adults about current foreign events and promote cultural understanding. One technique used by several large U.S. corporations is the Great

Decisions program, which uses a structured dialogue format to stimulate foreign policy discussions among co-workers. These efforts, when paired with discussions of the company's global operations and goals, might help managers and front-line workers communicate with each other better and think strategically about their own career and training needs.

6. ENCOURAGE ACADEMIA TO PURSUE INTERNATIONAL EDUCATION GOALS AND STRATEGIES

Although significant progress has been made in the past few years, few campuses—even business schools—have internationalized sufficiently to produce graduates with solid international skills and insights. Because of their emphasis on business training and continuing education, two-year and community colleges might be especially appropriate targets for assistance and encouragement to "go international." Institutions of higher education might also play a central role in bringing foreign languages, foreign studies and foreign exchange programs into elementary schools, high schools and vocational programs by coordinating curricula and lending expertise and administrative assistance.

> **B**ecause of their emphasis on business training and continuing education, two-year and community colleges might be especially appropriate targets for aid and encouragement to "go international."

7. REQUIRE UNIVERSAL, EARLY FOREIGN-LANGUAGE INSTRUCTION FOR CHILDREN

Foreign-language and cultural instruction need not be expensive if states are willing to utilize the wide talents and often voluntary efforts of foreign students, spouses and citizens in the community. This may require a willingness to waive the normal procedure for granting teaching certificates, but it has been done. North Carolina, for instance, which has the nation's highest rate of elementary school foreign-language enrollment, offers a temporary, two-year teaching certificate to nontraditional providers of language instruction. This is backed by an intensive but user-friendly certification program for foreign-language instructors.

8. FOSTER WIDER USE OF STUDENT AND FACULTY EXCHANGE AND STUDY-ABROAD PROGRAMS

Student and faculty exchange programs are common and well-established at major universities, and at high schools that serve students in relatively wealthy communities. These programs, however, involve too few citizens, especially from rural and minority populations. Moreover, smaller institutions rarely have the administrative resources required to identify good candidates, much less manage their predeparture training and financial applications.

As it is, most exchange programs are self-selecting, often benefitting the few well-to-do, globally attuned students, and only the faculty who can afford to ignore an extended stay's negative consequences on future tenure and promotion decisions. Moreover, although scholarships are available, with some even targeted to underrepresented groups, students often are not reached early enough in their schooling.

Crafting a supportive civic capacity for trade will be difficult unless orchestrated through a joint planning effort among public and private stakeholders at the state and local levels. Strategic planning can provide the impetus necessary for sustaining these costly initiatives—costly not so much in terms of tax dollars as in leadership resources and collaborative effort.

> **S**tudent and faculty exchange programs are common and well-established in some communities—but are insufficiently widespread to reach their potential for crafting a supportive civic capacity for trade.

CONCLUSION

Remember our hypothetical, irritated, state trade director who, at the outset of this book, demanded to know: "Who called the doctor?!"? The answer is that, in most states, no one has—yet. The more salient question, however, may be whether states can afford to wait for someone to make that call.

If we assume that the purpose of state economic development agencies and programs is to help businesses create family-wage jobs that improve economic opportunities for citizens, if we assume that competing effectively in the global economy is critical to business growth, and if we assume that for the foreseeable future public resources to achieve these objectives will be sharply limited, then business-as-usual does not appear to be an option. If state trade programs are to meet the challenges of the future with the resources of the present, if they are to overcome their problems of marginal impact, service fragmentation and inadequate accountability, then there seems little alternative but to re-envision their purposes, their practices and their partners.

> **I**f state trade programs are to overcome their problems of marginal impact, service fragmentation and inadequate accountability, then there seems little alternative but to re-envision their purposes, practices and partners.

Building "The International State"

Making the shift from trade *promotion* to trade *development* is not a matter of semantics; it is a fundamental change in purpose and approach.

For more than a decade—in some cases, much longer—state trade promotion programs have worked, often against great odds, to promote exports. The fact that they have accomplished as much as they have is more a testimony to their determination than it is to the political or budgetary support they have received. And yet promotion—that is, moving domestic goods into overseas markets—is only one component of the much larger, more complex challenge of trade development. The objective of trade development is to foster market-savvy firms that continuously adapt their products, operations and business alliances to compete effectively, and at global levels of quality, in both home and foreign markets. It involves exports, imports, joint ventures, investment and much more.

And small- and medium-sized businesses—which offer the greatest potential for trade-related growth and, typically, are the clients of state development programs—require trade development help. A one-stop-shop system that simplifies access to available public and private services is a step in the right direction, but it is not enough. For one thing, these firms need much more: peer contacts, access to quality private business services (experienced international bankers, lawyers, accountants, trade consultants), market data, transportation and communication infrastructure, and help with product design, production, packaging, workforce development and finance, to name but a few. For another, many existing services are inadequate to the task. The private marketplace often does not—and, in many cases, will not—provide this help to such firms, especially in the nation's more isolated rural and disadvantaged communities. The public sector (local, state and federal) has limited resources to do so. And non-profit organizations typically lack sufficient expertise as well as resources.

Making the shift from trade promotion to trade development is not a matter of semantics; it is a fundamental change in purpose and approach.

The prospect of restructuring this struggling and ill-connected amalgam of trade service providers into a coherent trade development system is not a threat to trade service providers; it is an opportunity of the first order. It is an opportunity to sort out their core competencies, strengthen them, and draw them together to serve businesses with trade growth potential. It is an opportunity to provide American businesses with the range and quality of export assistance services that are commonly available to their competitors in major industrial nations throughout the world, but only partially available here. It is, in addition, an opportunity to establish trade development as a full-fledged discipline in the field of economic development—one characterized by professional standards for programs and practitioners, robust dialogue, interdisciplinary alliance, and a solid foundation of data, research, best practices and institutional memory.

It is, in short, an opportunity to create *The International State*—a state characterized by a vigorous, deeply-integrated, public-private trade development system, a growing capacity to manage state international affairs and interests, and a populace aware of and capable of taking advantage of international opportunities.

State officials, eager to serve their customers better, often seek "models" of successful programs developed elsewhere that they might use themselves. But models typically do not cross borders very well. Economic conditions, business services infrastructure, industry structure, trade prospects and available resources differ markedly from state to state. Consequently, this book does not present a "model" for creating a comprehensive state trade development system. Instead, this book outlines the principles that should guide efforts to design such a system and provides examples, where they exist, of efforts to carry out one or more of these principles. How—and even whether—states and their private and non-profit trade services partners choose to turn these principles into an operational system will vary. *(See Figure 12, Building the International State, on pages 140-142, for a summary of the goals, principles and process tools discussed in this guide.)*

> **T**he prospect of restructuring the struggling, ill-connected amalgam of trade service providers into a coherent trade development system is not a threat to trade service providers; it is an opportunity of the first order.

Filling the Knowledge Gaps

Even if they do work toward the goal of internationalizing their economies, states will be hamstrung unless better information is collected and made available across a range of issues:

■■ *Useful information about current exporters.* Basic information at the state and local level about which firms export, how often, to what markets is still largely unavailable, as is knowledge about the day-to-day hurdles these exporters face. Because these firms are already motivated to trade, they represent the greatest potential for near-term growth, if public and private sector organizations can help them succeed. Knowing more about them is critical.

FIGURE 12. BUILDING THE INTERNATIONAL STATE

GOAL: ALL COMMERCIAL SECTORS ENGAGED IN INTERNATIONAL COMMERCE

- Business managers think strategically about global markets

- A firm's decision not to export is a conscious and logical choice

- Competitive manufacturing and service companies have ready access to quality trade-assistance services and export financing

OBJECTIVES AND DESIGN PRINCIPLES

OBJECTIVE 1: A VIGOROUS TRADE DEVELOPMENT SYSTEM (DEEPLY INTEGRATED, PUBLIC-PRIVATE)

WHAT TO AIM FOR:

- A strategic and widely shared vision

- A "second generation" of international business services

- Strong corporate champions

- Customers take an "equity position" in the trade development system

- Deep partnerships across political boundaries and disciplines

- Innovation and continuous improvement

HOW TO STAY ON TRACK:

- Clearly articulate trade development objectives and operating principles

- Improve long-term strategy development to anticipate shifts in global markets

- Think in terms of supply and demand for types of services, rather than checklists of program activities and events

- Base services on client-articulated needs

- Mobilize existing service providers, rather than provide all services directly

- Use open and disciplined competition for public funding of trade programs

- Help industrial sector organizations take responsibility for changing business behavior

- Ensure that trade assistance services are available to firms in rural and disadvantaged communities

- Use market mechanisms like fees for services, commissions, and soft loans

- Measure, and base program funding upon actual outcomes

- Encourage program innovation

140

OBJECTIVE 2: A CAPACITY TO MANAGE FOREIGN AFFAIRS

WHAT TO AIM FOR:

- A mechanism to anticipate and respond to changes required by international treaties and shifts in federal policy

- A clear identity abroad

- A means to cultivate trade relationships systematically

- Active participation in federal advisory bodies and other policy forums

- Awareness and active use by public agencies of United Nations and other foreign informational resources

- Federal financial and personnel resources for international trade, education and cultural enhancement identified and made generally accessible

HOW TO STAY ON TRACK:

- Develop an "intelligence center" for international affairs and a mechanism for disseminating information & analysis

- Maintain a directory of resident experts and nonresident natives in key international institutions

- Train leadership in basic trade policy & state trade history

- Build a positive image with foreign students and visitors, beginning with identification of red tape and simple barriers

- Identify and support resident foreign ethnic enclaves

OBJECTIVE 3: A SUPPORTIVE CIVIC CAPACITY FOR GOING GLOBAL

WHAT TO AIM FOR:

- Communities involved in a wide array of business, cultural and charitable activities overseas

- Productive international contacts for isolated business communities

- Voter understanding and support of two-way trade and investment

- A general public with personal contact, both at home and abroad, with foreigners who are their peers

- Fully internationalized curricula and student life

(continued on next page)

HOW TO STAY ON TRACK:

- Build civic involvement in international affairs

- Encourage and coordinate civic involvement in charitable activity abroad

- Support civic exchanges involving poor rural or inner city communities

- Educate and train community leaders in basics of trade

- Encourage local media coverage of foreign economic and cultural affairs

- Promote workplace-based training in global affairs

- Encourage academia to identify international education goals and strategies

- Insist on universal and early foreign-language instruction

- Foster wider use of student and faculty exchange and study abroad programs

PROCESS TOOLS: STRATEGIC PLANNING

ONE-TIME VISIONING PROCESS

QUALITIES:

- Private sector co-leadership
- Comprehensive

- Institutional mapping
- Grassroots involvement

ACTIVITIES:

- Analyze customer needs
- Assess regional capacities

- Identify mission statements
- Challenge assumptions

PERMANENT RESEARCH CAPACITY

QUALITIES:

- Higher-order research

- Accessible to all agencies

ACTIVITIES:

- Continue strategic planning
- Research the customer

- Perform dissemination function
- Develop partnership protocols

- Staff diplomacy function
- Staff coordination effort

- Staff annual provider's forum

MEANINGFUL PROGRAM ACCOUNTABILITY

QUALITIES:

- Supra-agency in design

- Well-funded evaluation

ACTIVITIES:

- Perform benchmarking
- Develop unified budget

- Track & assess NGO funding

- *How to export through intermediaries.* Many firms export products indirectly through intermediaries—wholesalers, trading companies, brokers, original equipment manufacturers, among others—rather than directly. Too little is known about the conditions that warrant using an intermediary, much less the comparative advantages and effectiveness of the various intermediary choices.

- *How to export services.* Many firms directly export *services*—financial, accounting, design and engineering, entertainment, and the like—rather than products. Yet little information is available to firms and practitioners on how exporting services differs from exporting tangible goods and products, much less on best practices for strengthening this sector.

- *Special export needs of specific industries.* Every firm operates within a specific industry. An understanding of the internal operations of the types of firms within a particular industry and the dynamics between interdependent firms in that industry might offer export developers a new

Until we begin to collect better information about trade-related issues, public and private trade services providers are, if not actually playing in the dark, then at least working on a very dimly lit stage.

143

window for helping firms. A sector-based approach might enable states to tailor their export development efforts around the specific needs and opportunities of the industry and, at the same time, achieve better scale.

■■ *Tested models for integrating business services and export development services.* For non-exporters, the principal barriers to internationalization are inside the firm, not outside in the marketplace. In much of Europe, export development services are fully integrated with other business service programs to strengthen the management skills and technological sophistication of firms and their owner/managers. The tendency of state export promotion programs in this country to be separate and distinct from other state business development services sharply reduces their ability to help non-exporters gain the skills they need to overcome their own internal limitations.

In these days of federal fiscal stress, states may have to take charge of developing a trade-related research agenda and funding it with the help of universities, foundations and others.

■■ *Collaboration models.* Public, private and non-profit sector trade assistance resources are severely limited. The need to stretch these resources through interfirm collaboration (for example, export networks) and interstate collaboration (such as regional trade programs) is great. There are relatively few examples of such collaboration as yet—even though collaboration is no longer a political nicety; it's an economic necessity.

Unless and until we begin to collect better data, intelligence and lessons about these and other trade-related issues, public and private trade services providers are, if not actually playing in the dark, then at least working on a very dimly lit stage. In these days of federal fiscal stress, when data collection and research efforts are among the first cut, states may have to add to their portfolio and take charge of developing this research agenda and funding it through collaborative efforts with universities, foundations and others.

Calling the Doctor

This book does several impolitic things. It critiques state trade offices even as it argues forcefully on their behalf. It points out that private and non-profit sector trade service providers, whom some claim should provide the services state governments now do, are often poorly equipped to do so (and, in some instances, flatly unwilling); yet it argues that they must be more fully integrated into a statewide system. It reveals that rural businesses are especially ill-served by trade assistance services, knowing full well that most providers' resources are already overstretched serving existing customers. And it demands that elected officials think beyond short-term, high-visibility trade events to a long-term, high yield trade development strategy.

In short, this book points out symptoms and suggests potential remedies. Whether or not someone ever "calls the doctor" is entirely up to the states themselves.

ENDNOTES

Full citations for all endnotes can be found in the references beginning on page 151.

[1] Robertson and Rindal.

[2] National Governors' Association.

[3] *Clearinghouse on State International Policies*, 2.

[4] Bremer.

[5] Germany, with an economy only about one-fourth as large, has occasionally edged the United States out of first place in total export value.

[6] U.S. Department of Commerce, *A Profile of United States Exporters.* The figure excludes reexports of foreign merchandise, services exports, and firms without at least one export shipment valued above $1,500.

[7] U.S. Department of Commerce, *A Profile of United States Exporters.*

[8] Richardson and Rindal, 1.

[9] Bremer, 2-3.

[10] For a quick summary of recent surveys of SME exports, see *The Exporter*, 2-3.

[11] Bremer, 2-3.

[12] U.S. General Accounting Office. See also International Monetary Fund.

[13] Trade Promotion Coordinating Committee, iv.

[14] Bureau of National Affairs, September 2, 1992, 1549.

[15] U.S. General Accounting Office, 24.

[16] U.S. General Accounting Office, 24.

[17] Stroh, telephone interview.

[18] Richardson and Rindal, 1.

[19] Swamidass.

[20] Trade Promotion Coordinating Committee.

[21] Office of the U.S. Trade Representative, "NAFTA Notes."

[22] U.S. Department of Commerce, *Business America,* 39.

[23] Bureau of National Affairs, June 30, 1993, 1081.

[24] Council on Competitiveness, 3.

[25] Richardson and Rindal.

Full citations for all endnotes can be found in the references beginning on page 151.

[26] Nothdurft, *Going Global,* 2.

[27] For examples, see Liner, 5.

[28] Stroh, "Fishing...," 3.

[29] For a more detailed description, see Bonnett, 17-23.

[30] Bonnett, 26.

[31] State trade office staff interviewed included persons in Colorado, Idaho, Iowa, Kansas, Minnesota, Montana, Nebraska, New Mexico, Oklahoma, Oregon, Texas and Washington.

[32] For a thorough review of European efforts to analyze the internationalization of small and medium-sized enterprises (SMEs), see European Network for SME Research. Part B of the report addresses the internationalization of SMEs. The network (of European research institutes) was established by the Commission of the European Communities and is coordinated by EIM Small Business Research and Consultancy, P.O. Box 7001, 2701 AA Zoeterneer, The Netherlands, fax: 31-79-415-024.

[33] Although new data will soon be available, state-level export figures have been notoriously unreliable and state-specific import data nonexistent. State "balance of trade" and other indices of state trade performance are often misleading; they are estimates of state shares of national trade activity based upon rudimentary assumptions about each state's industrial profile.

[34] *Clearinghouse on State International Policies,* May 1992, 1.

[35] National Association of State Development Agencies.

[36] National Association of State Development Agencies.

[37] Levine.

[38] The survey also found that 11 percent of firms surveyed cited "lack of information" as a barrier to export development; 9 percent claimed they had no time to pursue exporting (even if they were interested); and 34 percent simply expressed "disinterest" in exporting.

[39] National Association of State Development Agencies, 40.

[40] Levine and Vanderbrande, 43-46.

[41] Erickson, 2.

[42] International Trade Finance Report, 8.

[43] California Senate Office of Research, 20.

[44] *Clearinghouse on State International Policies,* November-December, 1994, 3-4.

[45] Twenty-four services were listed in the survey; the top ten fell into three categories: Information Services (how-to information, product market information, country market information and counseling); Buyer Contacts (trade leads, referrals to service providers, trade show support); and Trade Mechanics (training, shipping, product design).

[46] Corporation for Enterprise Development, *Restructuring Rural Business....*

[47] Cortright, 4.

Full citations for all endnotes can be found in the references beginning on page 151.

[48] Cortright, 5.

[49] Nothdurft, "The Exporting Game," 57.

[50] National League of Cities.

[51] Edison Electric Institute.

[52] See Edison Electric Institute. The Institute, which represents investor-owned electrical utilities, is located at 701 Pennsylvania Avenue, NW, Washington, DC 20004.

[53] Clearinghouse on State International Policies, 3-4.

[54] International Committee of the North Carolina Board of Science and Technology, 7-8.

[55] Osborne and Gaebler.

[56] Cortright, 11-14.

[57] Tradenz.

[58] Osborne and Gaebler.

[59] Source of principles: Osborne and Gaebler.

[60] Corporation for Enterprise Development, *Rethinking Rural Development*, 46.

[61] Ford. Personal interview.

[62] Christensen.

[63] DeMund.

[64] Smith.

[65] A survey conducted by the Wisconsin Export Strategy Commission supports this conclusion, as do the results of the much larger Kenan Institute study.

[66] Mostardi, 9-10.

[67] With permission,this description was drawn from the May/June 1994 issue of *Firm Connections*, a newsletter published by Regional Technology Strategies, Inc.

[68] Martinussen, 2.

[69] Glasmeier, Kays and Thompson; and Nothdurft, *Looking Beyond the Horizon*.

[70] Nothdurft, *Looking Beyond the Horizon*.

[71] Ford. Telephone interview.

[72] Cortright, 19-20.

[73] Doyle.

[74] Nothdurft, "The Exporting Game," 57.

[75] Smith.

[76] Cunningham.

THE INTERNATIONAL STATE: CRAFTING A STATEWIDE TRADE DEVELOPMENT SYSTEM

Full citations for all endnotes can be found in the references beginning on page 151.

[77] Hurlbert.

[78] Doyle.

[79] Doyle.

[80] Corporation for Enterprise Development, *Rethinking Rural Development*, 50.

[81] Doyle.

[82] Export Assistance Center of Washington.

[83] Ford. Telephone interview.

[84] Shuman.

[85] Bureau of National Affairs, July 13, 1994, 1104.

[86] Bureau of National Affairs, July 20, 1994, 1151.

[87] Cook, 3.

[88] Schill.

[89] This description is drawn from the lead article published in the Clearinghouse on State International Policies, February-March 1994.

[90] Bureau of National Affairs, "U.S., EU Disagree...," 31.

[91] Lueck.

[92] Southern Growth Policies Board, 2.

[93] Bremer.

[94] Althen. 59.

[95] In its early design stages, the Kentucky World Trade Center considered locating its facilities within a large cultural complex of theaters and artistic displays.

[96] *Clearinghouse on State International Policies,* July 1993, 2.

[97] *Clearinghouse on State International Policies,* May 1994, 1.

[98] Southern Governors' Association.

[99] *Clearinghouse on State International Policies,* January 1994, 3-4.

[100] *Clearinghouse on State International Policies,* June 1994, 4.

[101] St. John.

[102] For suggestions on how to build positive relations with the media, see Southern Growth Policies Board.

REFERENCES

Althen, Gary. "Cultural Differences on Campus." *Learning Across Cultures.* NAFSA: Association of International Educators. 1994.

Bonnett, Thomas W. *Strategies for Rural Competitiveness: Policy Options for State Governments.* Washington, D.C.: Council of Governors' Policy Advisors. 1993.

Bremer, Dr. Jennifer. *A Report Card on Trade: Evaluating Support Services for American Exporters.* Washington DC: Kenan Institute of Private Enterprise. February 1995.

Bremer, Dr. Jennifer. *Trading Up: Report on a Symposium to Provide State and Private Sector Input into the National Export Strategy.* Washington DC: Kenan Institute of Private Enterprise. September 1993.

Bureau of National Affairs. "Also in the News." *International Trade Report.* July 20, 1994.

_____. *International Trade Reporter.* September 2, 1992.

_____. *International Trade Reporter.* June 30, 1993.

_____. "Japanese Apple Growers, Researchers Protest Move to Allow U.S. Apple Imports." *International Trade Reporter.* July 13, 1994.

_____. "U.S., EU Disagree on Scope of Public Procurement Pact." *International Trade Reporter.* January 5, 1994.

California Senate Office of Research. *Tapping New Markets.* September 1993.

Christensen, David (Administrator, Division of International Business, Idaho Department of Commerce). Speech given at the National Association of State Development Agencies international trade directors meeting, Oklahoma City. 1994.

Clearinghouse on State International Policies. August 1993.

_____. February-March 1994.

_____. "The Fact Sheet." January 1994

_____."Factoring Immigrants into State and Local Trade and Competitiveness Strategies." June 1994..

_____."Kenan Institute Survey Finds Export Credit Gap." January-February 1995.

_____. "The Latest News." May 1992.

_____. "The Latest News." July 1993.

_____. "The Latest News." May 1994.

_____."Survey: Where Exporters Go For Advice." November-December 1994.

Cook, Lauren. "Commentary: Rebuilding Governance Structures in Central Europe...and the United States." *Clearinghouse On State International Policies.* February 1992.

Corporation for Enterprise Development. *Restructuring Rural Business Development Programs.* Washington. DC. March 1993.

_____. *Rethinking Rural Development.* Washington, DC. 1994.

Cortright, Joseph. *Reinventing Economic Development: Ten Ideas for Market-Driven Approaches to Promoting Industrial Competitiveness.* Staff Report to the Oregon Joint Legislative Committee on Trade and Economic Development. October 1994.

Council on Competitiveness. *Challenges.* December 1993.

Cunningham, Peter (Nevada Trade Director). Speech at the National Association of State Development Agencies annual trade directors meeting, Oklahoma City. 1993.

DeMund, Jeanne Cobb (Director, Trade and Market Development, Washington State Department of Trade and Economic Development). Telephone interview. February 1994.

Doyle, Mike (International Division, Iowa Department of Economic Development). Telephone interview. March 1994.

Edison Electric Institute. *Guide to Developing a Utility Export Program and A Business Guide to the Exporting Process.* Washington, DC. February 1993.

Erickson, Rodney. "State Export Promotion: Program Evaluation and Improved Targeting of Export Firms." Research proposal submitted to the U.S. Economic Development Administration. June 1993.

European Network for SME Research. *First Annual Report: The European Observatory for SMEs.* 1993.

Export Assistance Center of Washington. Unpublished budget documents. 1993.

The Exporter. New York: Trade Data Reports, Inc. August 1995.

Ford, Glenn (International Trade Division, Oregon Economic Development Department). Personal interview. June 1993.

_____. Telephone interview. March 1994.

Glasmeier, Amy, Amy Kays and Jeffrey Thompson. *When Low Wages Aren't Enough Anymore: Prospects for Remote Rural Branch Plant Regions in the International Economy.* State College, PA: The Pennsylvania State University. August 1993.

Hurlbert, Eric (Washington State Department of Agriculture). Telephone interview. March 1994.

International Committee of the North Carolina Board of Science and Technology. *North Carolina and the World Community: An Updated Perspective.* Raleigh, NC. October 1994.

International Financial Statistics Yearbook 1994. Washington, DC: International Monetary Fund. 1994.

Levine, Jerry. "State Export Programs: The Case for an In-Depth Approach." Unpublished research paper for Mentor International (San Francisco). 1993.

Levine, Jerry, and Fabienne Vanderbrande. "American State Offices in Europe: Activities and Connections." *Intergovernmental Perspective.* Fall 1993-Winter 1994.

Liner, Blaine. "Early Returns." *Clearinghouse on State International Policies.* September-October 1993.

_____. *A Strategy for Increasing Exports from Pennsylvania.* Washington, DC: The Urban Institute. April 1993.

Lueck, Thomas J. "Small City in New Jersey Goes After Global Trade With Help of Residents." *New York Times.* January 27, 1994.

Martinussen, Jeff. "More than an End in Itself: The Export Network as Stepping Stone." *Firm Connections.* Regional Technology Strategies, Inc. May/June 1994.

Mostardi, Stephen. "Finding Reassurance in Numbers: British Columbia's Flexible Networks." *Firm Connections.* Regional Technology Strategies, Inc. May/June 1994.

National Association of State Development Agencies (NASDA). *State Export Program Database.* Washington, DC. 1992.

National Governors' Association. *America in Transition: The International Frontier.* 1989.

National League of Cities. *Global Dollars, Local Sense: Cities and Towns in the International Economy.* Washington DC. 1993.

Nothdurft, William E. "The Exporting Game." *Governing.* August 1992.

_____. *Going Global: How Europe Helps Small Firms Export.* Washington, DC: The Brookings Institution. 1992.

_____. "It's Time the U.S. Got Serious About Exporting." *Northwest Report.* January 1993.

_____. *Internationalizing Rural Economies: Problems, Principles and Practice.* Washington, DC: The Aspen Institute. Forthcoming.

Office of the U.S. Trade Representative. "NAFTA Notes." Washington, DC. September 30, 1993.

Osborne, David, and Ted Gaebler. *Reinventing Government: How the Entrepreneurial Spirit is Transforming the Public Sector.* Reading, MA: Addison-Wesley. 1992.

Ouida, Herb. "Xport." *Economic Development Commentary.* National Council for Urban Economic Development. Fall 1992.

Richardson, J. David, and Karin Rindal. *Why Exports Really Matter.* Washington, DC: The Institute for International Economics and the Manufacturing Institute. July 1995.

St. John, Kathy (Executive Director for Development, Foreign Policy Association). Telephone interview. March 1994.

Schill, Katherine (budget analyst, Ohio Legislative Budget Office). Telephone interview. August 1993.

Shuman, Michael. "What the Framers Really Said about Foreign Policy Powers." *Intergovernmental Perspective.* Spring 1990.

Smith, Morgan (Colorado International Trade Office). Telephone interview. February 1994.

Southern Governors' Association. *International Education: Cornerstone to Competition.* Report of the Advisory Council on International Education. November 1986.

Southern Growth Policies Board. "Is the Press Watchdog Really A Housecat When it Comes to International Trade?" *Alert.* 1992.

Stroh, Leslie (editor and publisher, *The Exporter* magazine). Telephone interview. June 1993.

_____. "Fishing Where the Fish Are." *Clearinghouse on State International Policies.* July 1993.

Swamidass, Paul. *Technology on the Factory Floor II.* National Association of Manufacturers. 1995.

Trade Promotion Coordinating Committee. *Toward a National Export Strategy.* First report to Congress. September 1993.

Tradenz, New Zealand Trade Development Board. *Stretching for Growth: Building an Export Strategy for New Zealand.* 1993.

U.S. Department of Commerce. "U.S. International Trade Facts," *Business America.,* World Trade Week, 1993 Edition.

_____. *A Profile of United States Exporters.* September 1993.

U.S. General Accounting Office (GAO). *Export Promotion: A Comparison of Five Industrialized Nations* (GAO/GGD-92-97).

Wisconsin Export Strategy Commission. *Wisconsin: The Trade State.* Report of the Wisconsin Export Strategy Commission. February 1995.

CAROL **CONWAY** is program director in the Chapel Hill, North Carolina, office of the Corporation for Enterprise Development, a nonprofit research and demonstration organization dedicated to expanding economic competitiveness, especially in low-income regions, through the use of customer-driven business and human resource development policies. Ms. Conway directs the Clearinghouse on State International Policies, which produces a monthly policy newsletter by the same name. Ms. Conway has spent most of her career in international trade, including nine years in senior positions with the Southern Growth Policies Board, and four years with the U.S. Department of Commerce in the Import Administration division of the International Trade Administration.

WILLIAM **E. NOTHDURFT** is a writer and independent public policy consultant based in Seattle, Washington. He has authored or co-authored dozens of state policy initiatives on economic development, workforce education and training, welfare reform, adult literacy, rural development, agricultural diversification, natural resource management and state development marketing and promotion programs. Recent books include *Going Global: How Europe Helps Small Firms Export*, published by the Brookings Institution, and *Internationalizing Rural Economies: Problems, Principles and Practice,* forthcoming from The Aspen Institute.

CAROL **CONWAY**
Corporation for Enterprise Development—Southern Office
1829 East Franklin Street, Suite 1200-M
Chapel Hill, NC 27514
Phone: 919-967-5300

WILLIAM **E. NOTHDURFT**
William Nothdurft Associates
312 Second Avenue, Suite 605
Seattle, WA 98119
Phone: 206-281-7702

THE RURAL ECONOMIC POLICY PROGRAM (REPP)

Established in 1985 at The Aspen Institute, the Rural Economic Policy Program (REPP) fosters collaborative learning, leadership and innovation to advance rural community and economic development in the United States. REPP aims to help rural decisionmakers better understand how local choices and opportunities fit into the larger economy, and to speed the adoption and application of public and private initiatives that will sustain rural progress and improve the lives of rural people. Headquartered in Washington, DC, REPP is funded by The Ford and W.K. Kellogg Foundations.

The Aspen Institute brings timeless ideas and values to bear on issues of practical leadership in today's world. It accomplishes this through nonpartisan seminars and policy programs designed for leaders in business, government, the media, education, and the independent sector from democratic societies worldwide.

For more information about REPP or REPP publications, please contact:

Rural Economic Policy Program
The Aspen Institute
1333 New Hampshire Avenue, NW, Suite 1070
Washington, DC 20036
Fax: 202-467-0790
http://www.aspeninst.org/rural

Or call REPP Program Assistant Diane Morton:
202-736-5804